DESERT QUEST

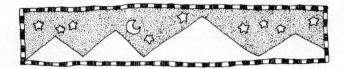

DESERT QUEST
The Hunt for True Gold

RANDOLPH JENKS and BEVERLY POWELL

Foreword by D. Elton Trueblood
Illustrated by Mark Herron

ZondervanPublishingHouse
Grand Rapids, Michigan
A Division of HarperCollinsPublishers

Desert Quest
Copyright © 1991 by Randolph Jenks and Beverly Powell

Requests for information should be addressed to:
Zondervan Publishing House
1415 Lake Drive, S.E.
Grand Rapids, Michigan 49506

Library of Congress Cataloging-in-Publication Data:

Jenks, Randolph
    Desert quest : the hunt for true gold / Randolph Jenks and
Beverly Powell.
        p.   cm.
    ISBN 0-310-53231-0 (pbk.)
    1. Sierra Madre Occidental (Mexico)—Description and
travel.
    2. Jenks, Randolph—Journeys—Mexico—Sierra Madre
Occidental.
    I. Powell, Beverly J. II. Title.
    F1340.J46   1991
    917.2—dc20   90–47739
                                                       CIP

Edited by Linda Vanderzalm
Designed by Ann Cherryman

Printed in the United States of America

91 92 93 94 95 / AM / 5 4 3 2 1

This book is for Julia, my beloved wife, and for the students who are too many to list, but whose faces are etched on my heart. I know them to be lawyers and doctors and merchants and workers, all solid contributors to both Mexico and the United States. They have enriched my life and have shared in my adventures. I rejoice to have known them.

This book is also dedicated to Wayne Powell, without whose support it could not have been written.

CONTENTS

FOREWORD

The story told in this book is unique. Though it belongs to the history of the Wild West, it is different from anything we normally encounter. Best of all, it is true!

In this account of the experiences of Randolph Jenks, south of the Mexican border, we learn of serious danger and of surprising success in dealing with a culture radically different from our own. Geographically, the scene is not distant, but culturally it is strangely alien.

The men who tried to find their way to a Mexican mine thirty-five years ago were often in real danger of being killed by desperate men who saw them as intruders. What is amazing to us now is the success that Pat Jenks and his friend had in *peacemaking*. What strikes me most is the way in which enemies were turned into friends. The story, as we contemplate it carefully, becomes an experiment in practical Christianity.

I have known the Jenks family for years, having been their houseguest in Tucson and a visitor to their cattle ranch. Now it pleases me to be able to help in introducing their book to you.

—D. Elton Trueblood

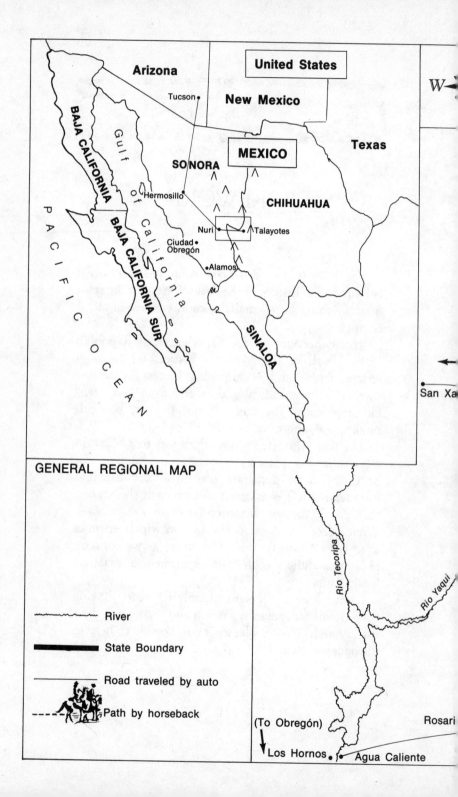

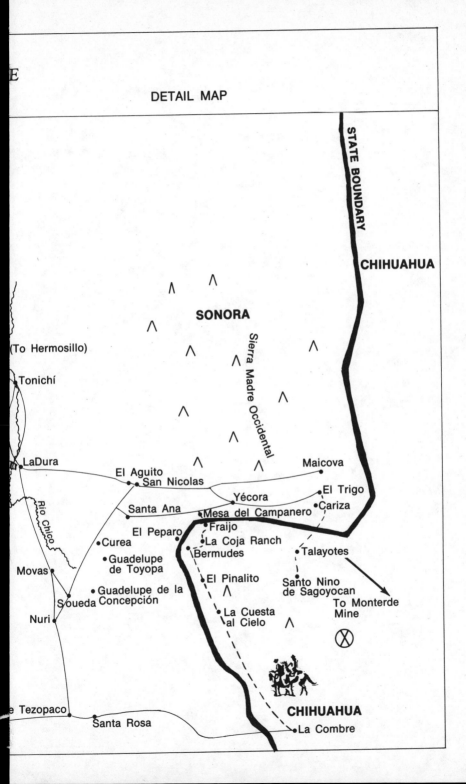

DETAIL MAP

STATE BOUNDARY

CHIHUAHUA

SONORA

Sierra Madre Occidental

(To Hermosillo)

Tonichí

LaDura

El Aguito

San Nicolas

Santa Ana

Yécora

Mesa del Campanero

Maicova

El Trigo

Cariza

Rio Chico

El Peparo

Fraijo

La Coja Ranch

Bermudes

Talayotes

Curea

Guadelupe
de Toyopa

Movas

Guadelupe de la

Soueda Concepción

Nuri

El Pinalito

La Cuesta
al Cielo

Santo Nino
de Sagoyocan

To Monterde
Mine

Tezopaco

Santa Rosa

CHIHUAHUA

La Combre

INTRODUCTION

Between 1935 and 1955, my family held the major interest in a mine in a remote area of the Sierra Madre mountains of northern Mexico. We had been a wealthy family until the stock market collapsed. Soon after that, my father was incapacitated by a stroke, leaving the family in greatly reduced circumstances. I was counting on the income from the mine to help me continue my education and obtain a Ph.D in ornithology, which was something I wanted to do very much.

Unfortunately, an audacious female bandit named Doña Poinciana had other plans for the gold bars from the mine. She robbed the mule trains so frequently that the mine was barely producing enough income to cover expenses. My trips to the Sierra began because of the need to find a way to transport the gold so that it did not cross Doña Poinciana's territory.

My family's mine, the Monterde mine, lay deep in the heart of the Mexican Sierra Madre, in an area so underdeveloped that it was accessible only by mule train. But this did not deter me. I was prepared by inclination and experience to undertake this search. I had camped in the wilds since I was a very young man, and I relished the adventure and challenge of finding a new route and outwitting Doña Poinciana.

I loved to explore, and I loved to be out in the wild. Even as a young child, when the other children at the Mesa Ranch School would be plotting a trip into town, I would be under a canopy of leaves, waiting to spot a new species of bird. This interest in birds stayed with me as an adult, and I seldom missed an opportunity to expand my knowledge.

My wife was not always sympathetic with my absences from home in the name of science, but in this instance, she agreed that I should go. And so the adventures began.

The Sonoran Thorn Forest stretches from the desert in northern Mexico to the mountains of the Sierra. The pine forest is so dense that the cowboys of the region invented the leather leg protection known as "chaps." To get to the mine, it was necessary to penetrate 100 miles into this unique botanical zone, some 150 miles inland from the sea, at a high altitude.

In my many attempts to approach the mine, I unexpectedly met with great personal danger, from both the local people and the elements. These journeys reinforced my faith in human nature as well as my deeply held conviction that violence is never the answer to problems between people. Having been raised in the Religious Society of Friends (Quakers), I lived by these beliefs.

I think often of the students who shared my adventures. They eagerly accepted the risks and shared with me the love for the outdoors and for the warmly hospitable inhabitants of the Sierra. These young people added a new dimension to my life.

Now, several decades later as I sit in the study of my retirement home in Alamos, Mexico, my adventures in the Sierra Madre echo in my memory. All of the characters you will meet in this book are real, and the experiences I have recorded actually happened. I have changed just a few details to allow the story to flow smoothly. I invite you to meet these extraordinary people and share these experiences with me.

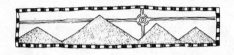

DESERT QUEST

CHAPTER 1

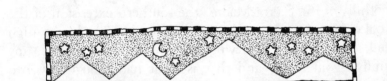

A Little Night Music

December 1951

I heard the sound clearly—the unmistakable metallic click of a weapon being cocked. It came from behind me, from the dense brush of the Thorn Forest. The night was so dark, I could see only a few feet—and that from the flickering light of the fire. We had left it burning to discourage *lobo*, the Mexican wolf that chose this moment to howl into the night, making my skin crawl at the wild, lonely sound of it. I heard a rustle in the bushes.

Don Needham, the student I had brought with me, had been asleep until he too was awakened by the click of steel

hitting steel. I could see his face, his wide, frightened eyes, then his arm sneaking across the stony ground toward his pack. He kept a hunting knife there, but it would not be a match for a gun already cocked and aimed. My pulse raced with fear.

We were in the heart of the Sonoran Thorn Forest, a dense and thorny zone of vegetation in northern Mexico, 300 miles south of the Arizona border. We had camped in the foothills of the Sierra Madre, the southern extension of the Rocky Mountains, which cut through Mexico like a high wall. Don and I were trying to find a western route to my family's gold mine, and that is what had brought us into Mexico, and into our present danger. I slid slowly out of my sleeping bag. I'm a tall man and didn't want to appear menacing to our visitor. "No, Don. No weapons. Let me talk to him," I whispered.

Don's arm stopped its stealthy movement toward the pack, and I exhaled with relief. My palms were sweaty as I lifted them into the air, hoping to show the intruder that we were friends.

My movement was met by another rustle in the brush, and I could smell the man now, and a sour smell of fear, discernible even over the tang of the wood smoke. I realized how crazy I had been to come down here. I regretted that my love for adventure now endangered not only my own life but also Don's. I thought about my wife and children. What would they do if something happened to me? I thought about the stories I had heard, tales of travelers who had come into the mountains of Mexico but had never returned. My thoughts raced. My mouth was dry.

"*Amigo,*" I called out in Spanish. "Come join us and share our fire. We have food . . . and music."

I heard a sharp intake of breath, but there was no answer.

"I'm getting the knife!" Don whispered.

"No. Get your guitar—but slowly," I said.

"My guitar!" Don said, his voice incredulous.

"Offer him some music. Trust me. Music works down here when words don't. Get the guitar!"

"All right," Don answered. I could see his frightened face as he crawled over to his guitar.

I raised my hands higher and called out again. "We have food and hot coffee. Come and sit by our fire."

Did the man even speak Spanish? Many people in these hills spoke Indian dialects, and my Spanish was basic at best. What had I gotten us into?

There was a long silence, punctuated by the screech of an owl flying over, hunting one of many rabbits that lived in the Sonoran Thorn Forest. My heart nearly stopped as the bird called out above us, and for a long time, or so it seemed, the only sound I could hear was my pounding heart.

I heard the sound of a foot crunching on the stony surface of the earth. The bushes parted and a man emerged, a slightly built man, with dark eyes that glittered in the firelight. I froze, hardly daring to breathe, and saw that he held a .22 caliber rifle in shaking hands, with its barrel aimed straight at my heart. In spite of the weapon, he looked more frightened than I was, and I prayed that his trembling fingers wouldn't accidentally fire the gun.

"Play a song, Don," I hissed.

"Okay," he answered, his voice shaking.

"I'm going to make some coffee," I said in Spanish. "Please, sit by our fire." I tried to sound relaxed. The barrel of the gun followed my heart as if held there by a string. Trying to ignore it, I moved slowly toward the water can. Still no music from Don. Instead, he was fiddling with the tuning keys.

"Play something!" I said again.

Our visitor's silence seemed more and more ominous as the moments ticked on. Finally a few tentative chords filled the air. "Pat! My mind's a blank! What shall I play?" Don asked, his voice now a wail.

The barrel of the rifle swung immediately toward him, and I saw beads of sweat popping out on his forehead, even though the night was cool.

"Try 'La Cucaracha.'" I went on filling the coffeepot, my hands shaking so hard that I spilled as much water as I poured into the pot. The man still had the gun aimed at Don. He looked at me with suspicion as I took a cheesecloth and poured some coffee onto it, then pulled the edges up and tied it closed with a string. I would have to move past the barrel of the loaded gun to get to the fire, so I motioned to him that I needed to put the pot on the rocks so it could heat. He backed away a few steps. Don was strumming now and starting to sing the words to the song. The man looked interested, and the barrel of the gun dropped a bit.

"Please, sit down. Rest yourself," I said to him in Spanish and edged in front of him to start the coffee heating. Except for the gun, he wasn't a fearsome-looking man at all. He was shorter than either of us and so thin that the bones on his face clearly stood out, revealing him to be Indian. Perhaps he was a Pima from one of the tribes that live high in the passes of the Sierra. The contrast between him and my fully muscled young college friend was striking.

The man's dark skin was covered by a layer of dust that looked almost gray in the light of the fire. He wore ragged and dirty pants tied at the waist with a length of cord. The night was cold enough that Don and I were sleeping in sweatshirts inside warm sleeping bags, but this man wore a thin shirt with many holes through which the wind blew. His pants didn't reach his ankles, and below them his feet were protected only by sandals made from a piece of rubber tire, tied on with leather straps.

Don found his voice and sang out with forced enthusiasm. For the first time, our visitor's face relaxed.

Cautiously, keeping an eye on our guest, I lowered myself onto my bedroll, leaned back against the rock, then patted the space beside me, inviting the man to sit down. His eyes narrowed with suspicion as he considered this, and I held my breath as I waited for his reaction.

It was a long moment, but he finally lowered the rifle and edged his way toward me. He cautiously settled down beside me.

"*Muchas gracias,*" he said, in a voice so high it was startling.

I exhaled. The danger seemed to be over.

We fed him several mugs of hot coffee and heated up the stew left over from supper. He ate every bit of it like a hungry coyote, and I wished we had more. Then I remembered a package of cookies. I dug them out, and we shared them.

"What is your name?" I asked him.

"*Juan. Mi nombre es Juan,*" he answered, his mouth still full of crumbled cookies.

In slow and careful Spanish I said, "I'm Randolph Jenks, but my friends call me Pat. This is Don Needham, my friend. What are you doing in the forest in the middle of the night?"

He wiped the cookie crumbs from his chin with a dusty hand. "My village is high in the mountains. My family died, so I thought I should leave. Since then, I live in the hills. I hunt for food and find plants to eat."

I digested this information in silence. I couldn't imagine such a solitary and nomadic existence. Don started to play one of the *ranchero* ballads, a long, mournful tale of lost love.

I leaned back against the rock as the sound of Don's music filled the night. Now and then my imagination would get the better of me. I imagined how Juan had gotten the rifle and ammunition. I would picture some other traveler, sleeping by his campfire . . . My wife says I'm too trusting, and I know she's right. I really didn't want to believe Juan was capable of harming another human being.

It was late December, and as the evening grew late, it got to be very cold. I invited Juan to share our fire and wondered how he would keep warm. We had brought only the two sleeping bags with us. Presently he got up and went into the bushes. He returned a few minutes later with a rolled-up blanket, a *serape* so dirty that its previously bright colors had faded to an even, mud color.

He wrapped the blanket around him and asked for more songs. We obliged. His dark eyes sparkled with excitement. The man was lonely, and I felt sympathy for him. Both of us sang along with Don, Juan in a high soprano voice, I in a deeper tone. The music resounded off the rocks on the one side of the clearing and into the trees and cacti that surrounded us on three sides. The fire crackled warmly and filled the air with the spicy smoke that only a mesquite fire can generate. We were three very different human beings— one a student, one a rancher with four children, and one a nomad of the Thorn Forest—yet a closeness developed between us as we shared the fire under the stars.

Our fire burned down until it was only glowing embers, and the moon vanished behind the high ridge of mountains. The stars were as brilliant as I've ever seen them, incredibly bright. The Milky Way covered the whole sky, or so it seemed, with a dense spattering of stars that shone more intensely than they appear in the city.

I threw another log on the fire as insurance against the

wolves, whose howls still pierced the cold night air. Exhausted, Don and I crawled back into our sleeping bags. Juan rolled himself tightly in his blanket and lay between us and the fire. One dirty arm still held the rifle, which had never left his side. He instantly fell asleep.

I raised my head and looked at Don, who was watching our guest with great suspicion, no doubt wondering if we would be murdered in our sleep. "Good night," I said, my voice low so it wouldn't wake up Juan.

"Do you think we're safe?"

"I think we'll be all right. We've made a friend of him, and that's better protection for us than a gun."

"I hope you're right," he said, unconvinced.

I slid into the downy bag and put my hands under my head, making them into a pillow against the rocky ground. Our trip might be harder and more dangerous than I had surmised. How many other solitary travelers were out there living in the forest? We still had over a hundred miles of rough travel ahead of us if we were to find a way westward to the mine. I wondered if we would make it. Then I slowly surrendered myself to sleep.

The next morning I awoke to a crackling fire. A red-tailed hawk circled above us, a heavy, fine specimen, and a covey of quail cried their mourning song into the crisp morning air.

Juan had risen earlier and had put some dried mesquite logs on last night's embers. He was quite happy with his efforts and pointed to the fire with a wide smile. He had emptied the dregs of the coffee and filled the pot with clear water. From a fold in his blanket he took out a packet of dried leaves and seeds.

"What do you call that?" I asked, curious.

"It is *hierba anís*. It makes a very good tea," he announced in his high, almost feminine voice.

"Looks interesting. I study plants and herbs. Did you find it near here?"

"No. Not very near. Higher, where the pines grow."

"May I have a little of it to take home with me?"

"*Sí, Señor*, of course. Here, look! I have others."

I eagerly listened as Juan described how each plant grew and how each was used by the people of his village. He gave me samples of the herbs, which I planned to give to a faculty member at the University of Arizona. My friend eagerly studies the medicinal qualities of each new plant as if it were a rare treasure.

After our conversation about the herbs, Juan's shyness vanished. I prepared bacon and eggs for breakfast, while he chattered on, the dam of his solitude broken. He told us all about the way he lived.

"I live in a cave when it rains, you know," and here he made lateral movements with his hands to indicate that it was a low, sloping overhang. "It is warm when I light the fire, and I can see the whole valley from there."

"But where do you get food?"

He shrugged. "It is no problem. Sometimes I earn a little money from selling animal hides, and once or twice a year I go into town for supplies."

Juan was as tough and wiry as the coyote whose skins he sold. "Last year," he said proudly, "I made twenty dollars by selling a pair of wolf cubs to a visitor from your country. He said they would go into the zoo!"

"The one near Tucson?"

"*Sí*. Twenty dollars bought me a big bag of beans and enough corn for the whole year." His smile was wide and his eyes happy at his success.

He served us each a cup of the licorice-tasting *hierba anís* tea. "*Hierba anís* is the best of them. I drink it every day," he confided, his face proud, as he urged us to drink ours.

Don and I looked at each other, and I knew he was thinking the same thing I was. Did the tea make our visitor's voice like that of a woman? Don didn't drink much of his either.

Breakfast over, we began to break camp. I stashed our equipment securely in the back of the jeep and recalled the story of some geologists who had come here several years ago—a story I had disregarded when I had heard it. Their jeep had been totally dismantled, leaving only the frame in the soft sand of a dry wash. Everything removable had been taken from it, and the men themselves had vanished forever. Not even their bones had been found.

Juan called a good-bye and headed down the trail. I backed up the jeep in a cloud of dust and set out to find the valley where the Monterde mine was situated, little realizing how long our journey would be—or how far it would take us.

CHAPTER 2

Trogons and Parrots

The rutted road we followed in the jeep wound around the sides of small mountains and climbed gradually as the hills increased in altitude. The air grew colder with each passing mile. It was hard going. We often had to stop and clear the road of fallen trees—victims of lightning or perhaps a windstorm. It was clear no one had traveled the road since summer. I had been told the road had been built by a timber company that used it to haul out logs from the Sierra. We were glad they had built it. Otherwise, there would have been no trail at all.

"I'm hungry, Pat," Don announced. "Let's stop for some chow."

"That looks like a good place." I pointed to the left where a small stream ran near the road. We pulled off the road and stopped beside the stream.

"I'll get the food basket," Don said and hurried to the back of the jeep to take it out. Soon we were lying back on a grassy bank, having a little rest and satisfying our hunger.

"Tell me about this mine, Pat. I never was really clear what the problem is."

"You're certainly entitled to know. That fright we had last night almost convinced me to give it up."

Don laughed. "It worked out all right. So what's with the mine?"

"In 1935, my family acquired an interest in the mine, and eventually they hired a friend, John Pope, to manage it. I know John well because he used to be my teacher when I went to Mesa Ranch School, where my parents sent me from my home in New Jersey because of my interest in the West."

"I realize we're trying to find a western approach to the mine, but why?"

"It's all because of Doña Poinciana."

"A woman? What does she have to do with it?"

"She's a remarkable woman. She's a bandit who rules with an iron hand over a gang of Tarahumara Indians. John tells me they're terrified of her and will do anything she says. Since John has been running the mine for us, she's been in control of the trail from the mine to Creel, the place where the railroad ends."

Don looked puzzled. "What do you mean, in control of the trail?"

"She robs the mule trains anytime she wants to. John says if he were to shoot her, he would have a Tarahumara revolt on his hands, and it would be impossible to find workers for the mine. He's sort of in a bind. Tarahumara territory covers the mountains only on the Chihuahua side of the Sierra Madre. John figures if we could get the gold out another way, we would start making a profit."

"You mean you're losing money on the thing?"

"Well, we aren't making any. Doña Poinciana robs so much of the gold that what is left is barely enough to pay for expenses."

"I see." He was quiet for a moment. "What's the woman like?"

"I hear she's quite something—a flashing-eyed, tall woman, who rides in a fine dress. Apparently she's descended from one of the *conquistadores*. John Pope tells me the Indians worship her, probably because she shares the gold with them. The whole tribe is desperately poor."

"Wow! That's quite a story."

"Don, I've been thinking about what happened last night. We could have been killed. I really didn't expect this trip to turn out to be dangerous. I'm thinking perhaps we shouldn't go much farther. I don't want either of us to come to harm."

"Come on, Pat. You've been in the hills in other parts of Mexico and nobody bothered you. Anyway, I don't think that guy last night really meant us harm. I think he was just hungry and scared at the same time."

"Perhaps."

"Don't stop now. The good part is coming up!"

I really didn't want to go back, but I was concerned for our safety. I wanted Don to be part of the decision. I was convinced by his arguments, so we started to gather up the lunch things to go on.

As I put the ice chest in the back of the jeep, I heard the cry of a bird and turned to see a parrot-like trogon, a rare bird with a long coppery tail. I ran for some binoculars and handed one pair to Don. As I focused on the beautiful bird, I could see its graceful, perfect colors. It sat on the branch of a pine tree and watched us, head cocked, as if it were more interested in us than we were in it.

"What am I supposed to be looking at?" Don asked, his face puzzled.

"A trogon. Look, up there, on the branch of the tall pine!" I was nearly hopping with excitement. Although I earn a living for my family in ranching, my first love is ornithology, and the sighting of this rare and exotic bird was a real event for me.

"Oh, I see it. It's pretty." He put the binoculars down. "You know, Pat, the birds I like are the ones I meet at school." He grinned at me.

I laughed. "Maybe so, but you'll see a lot of the other sort in these hills. This is wonderful country for birds. It's on the flyway from North America, so not only can we spot the birds that live here year-round, but we'll also see others that are migrating. Look! Over there! It's a western tanager!" Don dutifully turned to look at this red-headed yellow bird, but I saw he didn't really share my enthusiasm.

"We had better be on our way. I want to find a good camping place tonight—one that's a bit more secure. I don't want to be awakened by any more clicking guns."

"I agree with you there. Let's go!"

As we bumped along the road, I thought about how much I enjoyed spending time with people like Don, college students who are leaving their teens and beginning their twenties. It's an almost magical stage of turning points and experiences that can set the course of their lives. I had exposure to many such young people in my role as alumni advisor at Theta Chi fraternity at the university near my home in Tucson.

I had asked Don to accompany me on this camping trip

not only because he shared my keen sense of adventure but also because he spoke excellent Spanish as a result of living near the Mexican border with his parents. Don also played the guitar, and in Mexico, music was almost a second language.

We went over some really hard country after lunch. I doubt that we covered ten miles that whole day. Some of the gullies (called *arroyos* in Spanish) that crossed our trail were so sharp-edged that not even the jeep in compound gear could get us across. When we came to one of these, Don and I wearily got out of the jeep and reached for the shovels.

"We've got to make another ramp, Don."

"I just hope it doesn't rain while we're in the mountains. If it does, we will have to do this work all over again."

"From the look of that sky, it's going to do something," I answered. We were already wearing our jackets, glad for their warmth.

Moving rocks and dirt was heavy and time-consuming work, and we were not making the sort of progress I had hoped for. That worried me. We had scheduled only ten days for this first trip. I had commitments at the ranch waiting for me, and Don had to be back in class. At the rate we were going, it would take ten days just to get into the area where the mine was located, which was in the very heart of the mountains.

Before we had left Tucson, I had checked the best available maps of the area, and it looked as if it was possible to reach the mine through a series of canyons. The problem I saw now was time. We simply wouldn't have time for much exploration of possible routes unless we could get to the region more quickly.

We climbed back into the jeep and for a while made better time. The road climbed steadily, and as we went higher, the air grew colder. The sun disappeared behind gray clouds that seemed to be getting lower each minute. The jeep was enclosed with those plastic flaps that such vehicles had in post–World War II days, and it had a heater, which I put on full blast.

We occasionally saw the hoofprints of cattle. The trail, for it wasn't really a road, was now clinging to the sides of steep hills and sloped sharply to conform to the shape of the mountain. The hills around us were covered with scrub oak mixed with thorn trees and the long, multi-armed *hecho* cacti. A few rangy head of beef cattle temporarily blocked the road, and the sight of them encouraged me a bit. There must be a ranch somewhere in the area. Perhaps we could find shelter there and get some information about trails at the same time.

We hit a bump. "Ow!" Don said. "That one almost tossed me out. Maybe you had better slow down," he grumbled.

I felt a little sheepish. I had been pushing it pretty hard all day. I was hungry and tired from the jouncing myself, and my arms ached from wrenching the wheel over the rough road. "Let's go a bit farther. I'm hoping we'll come to a ranch before long."

"Okay. That makes sense."

"Besides, look at those clouds! The sky's getting darker by the minute."

We climbed for another hour, still occasionally seeing the hoofprints of cattle. The road rounded a bend at the top of a high hill. Below us in what looked like an old volcanic crater was a small, cleared valley surrounded by the rough log fencing used for Mexican ranch corrals. A log house stood in the corner of it, with smoke curling from its chimney.

A line of silent men sat on the log rail, their heads turning in unison when they saw the jeep. As we descended toward the gate of the corral, I could see that their faces were grim, almost hostile. They were dressed in the manner of the Mexican cowboy, and I guessed the hut was their line shack.

As we neared the corral gate, which was made of loose logs pushed through square-cut holes in the upright log posts, more men came pouring out of the little hut, making us seriously outnumbered. Each face we saw seemed more hostile than the others. This was not the friendly welcome I had hoped for.

"What now?" Don asked out of the side of his mouth.

"Keep smiling!" I said, making sure my own grin was as wide as possible. One of the men motioned for us to drive into the corral, and we did so. I pulled forward and shut off the engine. In the silence I heard some commotion behind us and turned to see two men quickly barring the gate behind us.

I felt distinctly uneasy at this. How would we allay their suspicions? Several of them were armed with rifles. Prickles of fear ran up and down my spine, and I thought of those missing geologists.

"I think we're trapped," Don said, his face pale.

"Maybe not. There are horses in here. They probably don't want them to get away."

"Pat. The gate was open when we topped the hill. They shut it only after we drove in."

"Hm-m," I said, hoping he was wrong. But I feared he might be right.

The men edged closer to us. A few flakes of snow whirled around us and hit their hard faces. These were rough men—sour, dirty, mean-looking. I took a deep breath. We could do nothing but try to make friends.

"Here goes," I muttered to Don and leaped from the jeep, a huge smile on my face. "*Amigos!* We bring food and music.

Please share it with us." I whispered to Don, "I'll get the chocolate bars and the picnic chest. You unpack your guitar."

"What?" he asked in disbelief.

"It's worth a try. They've been here a while from the looks of them. They've got to be in the mood for a party."

"All right." He went around to the back of the jeep.

"*Fiesta!*" I said, smiling broadly, pretending not to notice their lack of hospitality.

The men were closer now, and I felt myself start to sweat in spite of the chill in the air and the increasing snow. The pine woods were dark and ominous under the lowering sky. I suddenly felt far from home and safety.

I found the Snickers bars and began handing them out to the men. One of the men hesitantly reached out a brown hand to take the candy, and I felt relieved. Maybe it would work. I set down the bag of candy on the hood of the jeep and went around to where Don was trying to get out his guitar.

His guitar had fortunately been stashed on the top, but the knot that we had tied it on with wouldn't come undone. Don's fingers were shaking as he fumbled with it. In spite of the candy, most of the men came closer and several of the rifles were now aimed at us. I reached below Don and pulled out the food hamper. There was a large can of beef stew in it, and I hoped it would do the trick. I pulled it out and held it up. "Food! *La música! Fiesta!*" I said, holding my arms wide.

"This knot—it's not coming loose," Don said.

"Keep trying," I persisted. The men were close enough now that I could smell their unwashed bodies.

"I've got it," Don croaked, his voice hoarse with fright. He strummed a chord, and the sound of it stopped the men in their tracks. Puzzled looks replaced the hostility on their faces. I began to breathe again.

"What shall I play?" Don muttered.

"Try 'La Cucaracha' again, then ask them what they want to hear."

At the first notes of the lighthearted song, the men relaxed. One of them picked up the bag of candy bars and held it out to the others. The men lowered their rifles, and a few men even smiled. The snow was thicker now, nearly obscuring the trees at the edge of the woods. I handed the men the can of beef stew and said, "Come, let's eat together."

The wind was rising. Don interrupted his song to suggest we go inside, and soon we were all sitting in front of the fireplace that dominated the small hut, sipping scalding coffee of a strength I had not encountered before.

"I'm Pat Jenks," I said to the man who appeared to be their leader.

"¡Mucho gusto! Enrique Álvarez here, and these are my sons, Roberto, Alvarado, Juan, and José María."

"I'm pleased to know you. Are all of these men your sons, then?" I said, glancing around at the group. "They do look like you." In fact there was a family resemblance among all of the men there. They were all tall, lean, bearded, and handsome. They wore rough denim pants and leather jackets lined with fleece.

Enrique gave a shout of laughter. "No, I do not have fourteen sons!" He seemed to think it a great joke and explained it to the others, who poked fun at him and speculated that a man such as he might well have fourteen sons. It seemed the others were cousins and that all had been at the line camp for three months, tending the cattle that grazed in the area during the winter. They considered the freezing weather outside mild compared to the high valley of their home.

The one who seemed the youngest, Roberto, heated our stew in an iron kettle and served it with a pot of beans they had had simmering on the stove. Then he prepared fresh tortillas while we watched. It was a real feast, especially when I went back to the jeep and brought in a bag of oranges, which the men treated almost reverently. I realized I had unwittingly given them a great treat.

As we ate, Enrique asked, "What brings you to our ranch?" The others fell silent, intent on my answer.

"We are trying to make a trail to the Monterde mine. Do you know it?"

He shook his head. "No. There are mines in the hills to the east of us. Perhaps it is one of them. The trails are hard this time of year. There is much snow up higher."

"We would like to go as far toward it as we can. It is high in the Sierra. Can you point us in the right direction?"

"Sí, Señor. We will lend you some horses, and Roberto can guide you, if you wish. The jeep will be useless. Perhaps you did not know, but this ranch is as far east as the road goes. From here it descends back into the valley, then goes to Yécora, and there it ends. Yécora is still very far from the Sierra. We call this place El Trigo, and it is from here you will have to base your journeys."

The room was silent for a moment. "We would appreciate your help."

"Tonight you will stay here with us, and tomorrow Roberto can guide you, if the weather permits."

"Muchas gracias. You are very kind," I said to him, grateful for his friendship and the offer of a guide.

After our conversation, the men went outside to tend the

horses, and Don and I unloaded our sleeping bags from the jeep.

"Why do you suppose they were so hostile when we arrived and then so friendly once the ice was broken?"

"I don't know. I suppose it's their isolation. A really bad guy could do them a lot of harm, and it would be a long while before anyone learned of it."

"Well, at least they're friendly to us now."

"That's the main thing. Come on, let's go back inside. It's freezing out here."

That night Don dived right into the conversation, and we played and sang until we couldn't keep our eyes open any longer. It was the sort of night that could not be imagined, with a wild storm howling outside and snow whirling in through the cracks in the walls of the shelter. The fireplace was a smoky one, and the air inside was dense from the smoke and the whirling snow. The chinks in the logs had long since lost their seal. Even so, we were safe, relatively warm, and well fed. When the time came, we placed our sleeping bags beside the fire, tucked closely in among our new friends. The company included a good number of fleas, but I was so weary I hardly noticed.

Once again we had met force with friendship, smiles, and music. Once again we had received friendship in return. I was encouraged. Perhaps we would be able to reach the mine after all.

Before the sun had risen I was awakened by moans from Don's bedroll. Alarmed, I sat upright.

"What is it?" I asked.

"Pat, I'm so sick. It's my stomach. Help me outside."

Don was pale and shaking, and when he came back in from the cold, his face was a picture of misery. To those who have never suffered from the dysentery that occasionally afflicts the traveler to Mexico, I can only say that you should be grateful.

It was too soon for him to be ill from the food we had eaten the night before. Our worried hosts had all gotten up at the racket we made and looked on anxiously as poor Don suffered in the snow, unable because of the severity of the attack to return to his bedroll. In all my travels I seemed to be immune to dysentery, and I had no medication with me to help Don's symptoms.

"I've got to get you some medical help. We'll go first thing in the morning." Don nodded weakly. I was very concerned. People have died from this troublesome and embarrassing illness. I had shared with Don the rules I followed to avoid becoming ill, and I couldn't understand how he had become so sick.

Enrique's face was worried. "Take Don on to Yécora. It's closer than going back the way you came. *Señor* McMurray is American like you, and he has medicines."

"Which way is Yécora?" I asked.

"Keep on this road; then go left. It's the way we take our cattle."

"Thanks. We'll leave as soon as it gets light."

Our hosts pressed coffee and a tortilla on me, then helped me load up the jeep so we could leave as soon as the sky turned a lighter gray. The storm had cleared away, leaving the trees frosted with a wonderful sugar snow that I would have appreciated more under better circumstances.

"Oh, Pat, stop the car!" Don said soon after we had begun. So it went all day. He grew sicker every hour, suffering not just from diarrhea but also from nausea. Soon he was so weak I had to help him in and out of the jeep.

The road was the worst I had ever seen, incredibly steep and narrow, with crumbling edges and a canyon below us so deep that had I had a choice whether to go on or go back, I would surely have turned back. As it happened, I had no choice. For hours on end, the road was too narrow even to back up the jeep and turn around, so it was onward to Yécora.

Perhaps it was our frequent stops, but Yécora seemed much farther than the *vaqueros* at El Trigo had said it would be. Possibly to them a day's ride was near. The road descended steadily, and it grew noticeably warmer. Each time the jeep bounced, Don moaned.

The trip seemed endless. Finally we arrived at a good-sized town with dirt roads and small houses of wood and adobe, each with frosted flowers in the yard and a small garden patch. We were directed to a comparatively large adobe house at the edge of town, and there we met for the first time the man who would become my dear friend, Gordon McMurray, who liked to be called Mac.

"Come in, come in!" he said. I introduced myself and explained Don's problem. The house had no regular flooring but was instead built on hard-packed earth that on close inspection seemed to be moving. A horde of fleas attacked my ankles.

Mac lumbered out to the jeep, where Don was waiting. "Got '*la turista*'? Come on in. I have just the thing you need." He helped Don to a canvas cot. "I keep a supply of penicillin."

He went for the medicine. I breathed a sigh of relief. I hadn't realized how anxious I had been about Don.

Mac came back, hurrying in a peculiar, rolling walk. "Here, take these. You'll be better in a couple of days." His face expressed warmth and concern as he held the glass so Don could swallow the pills. When Don had collapsed weakly back onto the cot, Mac said, "I'll go now and fix you

some tea the Indians use. It will help your stomach some.
You've got to drink lots of fluid, and it seems like this is about
all that will stay down."

I followed Mac into the kitchen and questioned him
closely about the herb he used for the tea. It was made from
the bark of a desert bush, the *manzanilla*. The tea did seem to
give Don immediate relief.

That night Mac and I sat beside his fire and watched Don,
regularly giving him the herbal tea. Except for the fleas,
which made us pretty itchy, it was a very comfortable room.

I learned that Mac was the only American in this part of
the Sierra. "Why did you come here to live?" I asked,
curiosity overcoming good manners.

"I had a bad marriage. I wanted to get as far away from her
as I could. I guess I thought the memories would stay there,
but of course they came with me." He was silent for a
moment, but his eyes still held pain. "She turned my sons
against me, and I guess that's what hurt the most. After a
while there didn't seem any point in leaving here. I was able
to get a small ranch, and I make a living from it. The people
here are kind to me."

I watched Mac as he got up to give Don some more tea.
Mac was squarely built, none too clean, with a huge
stomach. He didn't exactly have a beard at that time, but he
wasn't clean-shaven either. He had faded blue eyes that held
a shrewdness that made me feel he was a good judge of
people.

"Bring your sleeping bag in. I've got another cot, but I'm
afraid the fleas are pretty bad. You can put the legs of the cot
in some kerosene if you like."

"Thanks. I'll be fine." That night I did set the legs of my
cot and Don's cot into small cans filled with kerosene. The
fleas tried to reach us but fell into the fuel and died. At one

point the flap of my bag touched the ground. Within minutes I was itching and slapping at the opportunistic little creatures who had found a ladder to flea heaven. After that I tightly tucked in all flaps and strings. No more free lunch. Even with the flea hordes held at bay, it was a long and itchy night.

We stayed three days, at the end of which Don seemed totally recovered. Since we had used up five days of our time, I doubted that even with the best of luck we could find the mine in the time left. Reluctantly we decided we had to head back up to El Trigo.

"The men at El Trigo offered us a guide. Do you think that would be a good idea?" I asked Mac.

"Enrique and his boys? They know the mountains as well as anyone."

"Good. If Don feels up to it, maybe we can at least follow the trails for a day or so."

"You know you will have to make another trip down to this area. You'll never find the mine in a couple of days."

I thought about this for a minute. "I could come back in the spring."

"I was hoping you would say that. Would you mind if I give you a list of things to bring me and some money? I sure do get needy down here." He had such a pitiful look on his face, I burst out laughing.

"I'll bring what I can. Now we'd better get on the road."

Mac's eyes shone. "Bring me medicines of any sort and all the clothing and food you can pack in. These hills are full of the remnants of the Pima Indian tribe. Their poverty is desperate. *Anything* you bring will be used—I promise you that."

Don and I loaded the jeep and set off down the road. "I'm sorry I ruined the trip," Don said.

"Don't worry. You didn't ruin anything. How do you suppose you got sick?"

He looked sheepish. "Do you remember when we stopped at the Chinese restaurant several days ago?"

"Yes."

"Remember when you told me not to drink the milk?"

"Yes, I remember that."

"Well, when you left to talk to those people from Canada, I drank it anyway."

"Oh. I wondered about that. I've worried about that place anyway. The parrot doesn't look too clean."

"It's the cook who isn't too clean."

We both laughed at the recollection of the cook, who wore a high, grubby white chef's hat and long chef's coat, stained with traces of many dinners cooked and served. Incongruous as the chef seemed, it was the parrot that caught the eye, because he rode on the chef's shoulder and swiped food from the plates as they were served.

"Well, when we come back in the spring, you can skip the milk. I'm glad in a way for the time with Mac. He'll save us problems in the future. He offered his house as a base camp anytime we're in the area."

"I still feel kind of bad about it."

"Nothing happens by accident. We're led where we're supposed to go."

"Well, here's hoping the trail leads to the Monterde mine."

CHAPTER 3

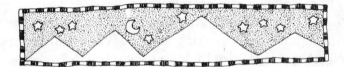

Into the Heart of the Sierra

The road back from Yécora went past El Trigo, so we simply retraced our steps. Snow still covered the ground around us. Now and then a melting clump fell with a *whump* audible even over the sound of the jeep's engine. Today we felt no time pressure, so both Don and I could enjoy the scenery and the sighting of many Mexican magpie jays, which reminded me very much of the legendary *quetzal* bird, with its long, streaming tail feathers.

Don felt much better and showed this by taking out his guitar and strumming it. He knew many songs of old Mexico, and taught me the words to some I didn't know. We sang as we drove along, enjoying the spicy smell of the pines.

As we climbed back up toward El Trigo, it grew colder, until our breath froze in the still air. We eventually came to the corral, and there sat Enrique, his sons, and their cousins on the top rail, as if they hadn't moved since our departure.

Their frowns changed to smiles as they recognized us. Quickly they tumbled off the rail to open the gate. This time we felt no fear as the heavy logs slid through the gate post and shut the opening behind us.

Enrique shouted a friendly greeting.

"Hola, Enrique. ¿Cómo está usted?"

"Bien, mis amigos, bien." He gave us an abrazo, the Mexican embrace of greeting and farewell. "And how is my young friend? Did Señor McMurray fix you up? Are you well?"

"Much better. Thanks, Enrique."

"So, now you want to take some horses and go into the hills?"

"Yes. That's exactly what we want to do. We don't have much time, but even a day or so will give me an idea of what the trails are like and how fast they can be ridden."

"Good. You will leave your jeep here and unpack some gear for the trail."

It was only noon. Our return trip from Yécora had gone much faster without the frequent stops the journey from El Trigo to Yécora had required because of Don's illness. I thought we could travel quite far that afternoon and hurried to unload some packs. With Mac's reassurances about Enrique's family, I had no second thoughts about leaving the jeep behind.

"Young Roberto will be your guide. He knows the hills well. Alone you would be lost."

We soon had our gear separated from the main supply and were ready to ride. The sleeping bags were bulky, but we rolled and tied them with some rope and fastened them behind the saddle. Each of us carried some food and other essentials in a canvas sack that we tied with a short rope to the saddle horn.

While we got ready to go, the *vaqueros* fixed us a hot meal of fried eggs, tortillas, and beans—typical fare for the Sierra, as we would later learn. We ate it with relish, then mounted up. Roberto insisted that Don take along his guitar. Don looked quite the authentic cowboy with his bedroll, canvas bag, and guitar. After saying good-byes to Enrique, his sons, and his nephews, we mounted our horses and set out on the trail.

Roberto led the way up a narrow trail into the dense forest of magnificent pines. A hawk soared above us, probably another red-tail. It was a peaceful woods, full of bird calls sung to a background of the wind sighing through the pines. Snow still covered the forest floor except where the sun had melted patches, exposing the dark earth.

An hour went by, and I noticed leaves curling up from the path, driven by a freshening wind. I breathed deeply of the cold air, enjoying the smell. I found myself almost hypnotized by the *clop-clop* of the horses' hooves along the narrow trail.

Much too soon the sky turned dark gray, and the air grew chillier by the minute. I anxiously looked at my watch. It was only afternoon—the darkness was coming from an approaching storm. Flurries of snow whirled through the woods, and I began to be alarmed. This was no place to be caught in a blizzard.

Roberto motioned for us to stop. His brown face was creased with worry. "We must find shelter. This grows very bad," he said in Spanish.

"But where?" I responded.

"There is a little *campo* ahead. We turn off this trail and ride for an hour. It's down in a little valley. Still the storm is coming fast . . ." The words trailed off, and he shrugged.

"Would it be quicker to go back to El Trigo?"

"*Señor*, I do not think so. We've been riding for four hours, and the *campo* is only an hour away. I think it would be better."

"Do people live there?"

"*Sí*, people live there. They're not friendly to outsiders, but they will give us shelter. We must hurry."

He spurred his horse and quickly trotted off along the rapidly darkening trail. Don and I followed, not wanting to spend the night in the open. If it weren't for our predicament, I would have enjoyed that ride through the woods, the blowing snow whirling around the tall pines. The trail slowly turned from mud into pristine white. It was quiet, except for the wail of the wind in the pines and the labored breathing of the horses.

It grew terribly cold. I wrapped myself in my clothes as tightly as I could, but we were not really dressed for a blizzard, wearing only jeans, sweaters, and jackets.

Soon the snow grew so heavy I could see only as far as Don's horse in front of me. I began to worry and finally called out for the others to stop.

Roberto rode back, and we huddled our horses together so our voices would be heard over the howling wind. "Roberto, how much further to this *campo*? I'm nearly frozen."

He looked down at his horse's head and seemed embarrassed. Flakes of snow frosted his dark eyebrows and mustache, and I realized my own face was numb from exposure to the freezing wind.

"*Señor*, I did not want to say it, but we are lost. I missed the turnoff to the *campo*. I don't know where this trail goes now."

"Then why are we riding on? It's nearly dark. We can't ride in the dark in this storm! We must find shelter somewhere."

"Sometimes, we put our horses where they will block the wind and lie down with the saddle at our heads to keep the snow off our faces."

"That sounds better than riding on as we have. Perhaps we can build a little fire."

"I don't think a fire will be much use in the storm."

"Let's see what we can find." We continued riding for a short distance through the fading light. "There! See that clump of trees? We'll shelter there."

"Good thing," Don said, his first comment for the past hour.

"I told you it could be an adventure, didn't I?"

"You delivered as advertised. I'm freezing!"

"Get your sleeping bag. We'll find the best shelter from the wind and crawl in them. I can't think of what else we can do. It's getting pretty dark to travel."

The trees, clustered together at the base of an embankment, seemed to offer some protection from the wind. In the shelter of the largest trunk, we arranged our saddles close together to block the wind from blowing directly on our heads. In spite of Roberto's advice, I tried to light a little fire, but it was no use. The wind blew it out repeatedly, and finally I gave up.

We tied the horses upwind from us. "Let's put our bedrolls together," I suggested. "That way our bodies will help keep each other warm."

"Like this?" Don said, laying his bedroll close against mine.

"Right. Here, Roberto. Put yours between the tree and mine."

We ate some biscuits from our packs and crawled into the bedrolls, trying to keep warm and dry. The ground was cold and hard and the wind howled louder.

I began to shiver within minutes of our crawling into the bedrolls, and within an hour I was shaking so hard it was painful. My legs particularly hurt. I fought back the urge to get out of my bedroll and run in the snow to work the tight muscles loose. This stage seemed to pass, and I grew very sleepy. It was this that alarmed me. Was I freezing to death?

"Don! Are you all right?"

"I'm all right. I seem to be getting warmer."

"Roberto! What about you?"

"I'm okay. It's my fault we're here. I will be okay, Señor Pat."

I wasn't reassured. It seemed to me that the snow was growing deeper on our bedrolls by the minute. That should have provided insulation for us, but somehow it didn't seem to be having that effect. Sleep began to seem so delicious I could hardly resist it, and I began to drift off. Then the thought of my wife at home with the four children came to my mind. "Julia!" I called, my voice ringing in the woods. My mind suddenly cleared, and I sat up. It was dark now, too dark to see the faces of Roberto and Don, even if they had been uncovered.

Frantic, I brushed the snow from the top of their sleeping bags and tried to shake them awake. It was only with great difficulty that I roused them, and by this time I was exhausted from the cold and the effort of it.

"Come on! We're saddling the horses. We've got to keep moving!"

"No, we need to rest. I'm really so tired, Pat. Let me sleep," Don said.

"It might be the last sleep you ever have. Come on! Get moving!"

Don grumbled and complained, but he saddled his horse. My fingers were so stiff with cold it took a long time, but finally I was ready. So were Don and Roberto.

"Let's go. Roberto, you take the lantern and lead the way. I'll be behind you and Don. I don't want one of you to drop back."

"Sí, Señor. I will go first."

"We'll try to make it back to El Trigo. It's our only hope to survive the night. At least the movement will keep us from freezing in our sleep."

We set off into the night. Our horses were as cold as we were, and the going was slow. The snow didn't seem to be falling as heavily as it had earlier in the night, and I could see the lantern ahead of me well enough to follow.

We had ridden for only a few minutes when Roberto suddenly pulled his horse to a stop and gave a shout of joy. "It's the turnoff!" he yelled.

"To the campo?" I replied, a surge of excitement reviving me.

"An hour's ride, Señor. It's the trail I told you about. I missed it in the snow when we passed before. The snow has let up, and from this angle I saw the rock that marks it."

"Yippee! Three cheers for Roberto. Let's go!" Don spurred his horse behind Roberto.

It seemed like a miracle. I turned my horse to follow onto the sharply descending trail. Within an hour I could see it widen as the dense woods that had been visible by the light of the lamp receded from the trail. We were in a clearing.

I'll never forget the sight of yellow light streaming onto the newly fallen snow, a beacon leading us to safety. The campo consisted of a few rough, log huts. The mud chinking was not too effective, and out of several huts shone golden rays of the lights within.

Roberto called out several times. In a low voice he said to me, "I must call out, otherwise they will shoot us. They don't like strangers here in Talayote."

"By all means, call out!" I muttered the words, wondering if John Pope could possibly appreciate the magnitude of his request for me to find a new trail to the mine.

Four men burst out of one of the doorways. It was immediately clear that we were highly suspect, in spite of Roberto's friendly greeting and explanations of our presence. One of the men, a one-eyed fellow the others called Ricardo, searched me and found a game-getter—a weapon used to collect bird specimens for study—under my jacket. From the look on Ricardo's face, I think he was convinced I had come to do him harm.

"It's to collect bird specimens. I'm an ornithologist," I tried to explain.

"It's a gun. I will take it." Having assured themselves that we would be able to do them no harm, they invited us inside to join the party.

Ricardo was a tough-looking man. One of his eyes had been put out somehow, and the lid draped across it, giving him the look of a pirate.

"Here, *tequila*," Ricardo said, offering me a cup of liquor.

"No, I'm not thirsty," I answered. I watched his good eye grow cold.

"You won't drink with us?" he spat out in Spanish. The room grew suddenly silent. I knew we were in trouble.

"Drink with them, *Señor*," Roberto urged in a low voice. "When you offend one of these mountain men, you don't walk away. There are many widows in the hills." Roberto's eyes looked at me, bright with alarm.

I thought quickly. Although I was not a drinking man, it seemed wise in this case to make an exception. I quickly told Ricardo I had misunderstood and would love to have some *tequila.* He handed me a cracked cup with a generous amount of the fiery liquor. I tried not to cough as I sipped it. The liquid sent warmth down my throat and into my stomach. I felt its effect ease away the tension of the past few hours and was grateful to my host for insisting that I have some.

Ricardo had seen Don's guitar. "Go get it. We have no music, and this is a *fiesta!*" Don, looking white and exhausted, went out to our horses and brought the guitar inside.

We sang for a while, but the smoky hut, *tequila,* and warmth were too much for me. I soon found myself nodding to sleep.

"Come, my friend. We have a bed for you." Ricardo took my arm and helped me to my feet. We went outside and took our bedrolls from the shed where we had left the horses. Then we crossed the snow-covered clearing toward a little hut where a fire had thoughtfully been built for us. The heat from the fire had melted the snow on the roof, and the roof itself leaked in a hundred places. We could find no dry place to escape the continual dripping, and the wind howled through the log walls. Still, it was far better than our beds had been in the forest, so we settled down to try to sleep.

Through the rest of the night, I got only an hour's worth of good sleep. I woke with a start and saw that gray light was penetrating the gloom. The fire was now as cold as the hut. I stretched within the sleeping bag, my body stiff with cold and cramped from the long, numbing ride of the day and night before. Thoroughly wet and exhausted, I felt almost sick from the ordeal.

Suddenly the light brightened. I heard the creak of the

wooden hinge as the door to the hut inched open and an old,
bent-over Indian woman dressed in a ghostly white dress
crept across the threshold. At most she was four feet tall, and
the lines of her face told of the hard life she must have
endured. Her silent entry reinforced the illusion that she was
a phantom, as she noiselessly crossed the room and laid down
a bundle that I supposed was intended to be our breakfast.

I lay very still, curiously watching her movements. She
stepped cautiously over our feet and approached the rough
fireplace. It was a ledge, really, protruding from the wall
where the edges of a flat, baked adobe shelf were wedged into
the depression between the logs, supporting the inside of it.
In the flat of the adobe, a hollow had been scraped out, and
here the woman built a fire. Soon it blazed up and sent a
welcome warmth into the room.

I sat up in my bedroll and gave Don's shoulder a poke.
"What?" he said, opening his eyes. "Hey, look! It's
stopped raining."

I motioned toward our visitor, and although we tried to
talk to her in Spanish, she acted as if we weren't even there.

Fascinated, I watched as she took an ear of corn, and
twisting it rapidly with one hand, she scraped off the kernels
with the thumbnail of the other hand. She ground these
kernels on a stone *metate* with the grinding rock called the
mano, and soon she had a pile of cornmeal.

She brought with her a bowl in which she mixed the
cornmeal with water, then patted it into flat cakes. A pot of
coffee then went onto the fire and heated up while she made
the tortillas.

By the time the meal was ready, we were hungry. And
when she offered us the tortillas, still smoking from the grill,
and hot coffee, we eagerly accepted and devoured the
delicious corn cakes. Mac had warned us about eating

tortillas made in the villages. He had said they often had living pinworms in them, but today pinworms were the least of my worries.

When we had finished the tortillas and sat back to drink a second cup of coffee, the woman silently left us, never having once met our eyes or answered the questions we had directed toward her.

More astonishing though was the way we felt within a few minutes of eating the food. Don looked at me in amazement. "What was in those tortillas?" His eyebrows were lifted with surprise, and I knew what he meant.

"I don't know! Whatever it was, it wasn't just corn." My blood seemed to sing in my veins, and I hadn't felt so strong since I was eighteen years old. All of my aches and pains had vanished, and I was filled with a sense of well-being. I felt wonderful, and I knew Don was feeling something unusual too.

"Did you see her mix them?" he asked.

"No, she was in the shadows, with her back to me," I said.

Don began jogging in place. "Wow! I feel like going for a run."

"Maybe these people have stumbled on something, an herb maybe."

"They live as people did in the stone age, but they sure know how to cook a tortilla!"

I nodded. My exhaustion had vanished, and I felt as if I had had a full night's sleep. I rolled up my bedroll, feeling that we should get back on the trail. I felt strong enough to tackle anything.

"If you could bottle that stuff, whatever it was, you'd make a fortune," Don said, as he packed his own sleeping bag. When we arrived at the other huts, we were surprised to see

Ricardo, up and tending the horses, apparently none the worse for his bout of drinking the previous night.

"Ricardo, what was in our breakfast? I study medicinal herbs, and that was a powerful one. I feel wonderful."

"You feel good, no?" He smiled at me, looking wicked.

"I feel terrific. What was it?"

"Only God's own good food."

I persisted, but he wouldn't acknowledge that anything had been in the food. He also refused to return my gun. It was with real regret that we rode away.

We returned to El Trigo before noon, and after saying good-bye to Enrique and his family, we set out for home.

"I'm sorry the trip is over," Don said.

"Want to come back in the spring?" I asked him.

"Yup. Just try to come without me."

"What about the danger?"

"I'm coming with you. We're going to find the trail to that mine."

"You've got a deal."

A view of the Sierra Madre.

A vista.

En route to Yécora.

The valley of Yécora.

Gordon McMurray of Yécora.

"Mac" in front of his cabin

Our jeep, bringing in supplies and medi-cines—on the road to Yécora.

A typical Pima Indian cave dwelling.

A Pima mother and her child

A Pima Indian shack.

A Pima family at the door of their shack.

The road to Yécora again. The jeep goes up a river bed in Arroyo Reparo on the road from Obregón to Yécora.

The author, Randolph "Pat" Jenks

Pat Jenks

The artist Gilberto Fierro on horseback.

In front of cabin at LaCoja ranch.

Starting out on horseback from LaCoja, Pat in front.

Leobardo Clark

Rough going on the trail

CHAPTER 4

The Orphan Boy of the Thorn Forest

When I told John Pope, the Monterde mine manager, about the results of my earlier trip, he urged me to try again, pointing out that the mine could not survive much longer at the rate things were going. "I really don't know if we can do it, John, but I'll try to get as far into the mountains as I can. Why don't you start someone out from the mine itself and have him head west. Perhaps he'll come to a town that I can link up with from my side."

"It's worth a try," he had said.

So in the spring of 1952, Don Needham and I returned to Mexico. In Hermosillo, we were joined by Jesús Lizárraga and Hectór López, both students at the University of Sonora. A friend had encouraged them to travel with us, suggesting they would benefit from spending time with me and a student from the University of Arizona.

"The trip may be hazardous," I said to Hectór and Jesús when I stopped to talk to them about coming with us.

"It may be less hazardous for you if we're along. Have you considered that, *Señor* Jenks?" Jesús said, his dark eyes serious.

"No, I hadn't. I just want you to be forewarned."

"I want to come," said Hectór, whose enthusiasm for the adventure increased steadily from that point.

Jesús was a talented linguist with an intelligent and far-reaching mind. He was a tall, lean, young man with an odd way of tilting his head when he looked at you. He seldom smiled.

Hectór López was just the opposite. He was much rounder in appearance and knew and played every song any of us had ever heard. His guitar case was always on his back, and he reminded me a little of a turtle.

The three young men became fast friends within an hour of our leaving Hermosillo. And so we were back again, trying to make the best possible driving distance every day. I hoped to have a full week on horseback, which would be sufficient to pack into the mine and out again, if everything went according to our plan.

The road between Yécora and Nuri was narrow, and to call it steep was an understatement. Mac had warned us that one portion of it was particularly dangerous, for it was used by the timber trucks coming down out of the hills. Once the trucks began their descent, they could not stop, and they skidded the entire downhill stretch with their brakes locked. Any vehicle coming up while they were coming down would be smacked off the road and into the canyon below. We now had to climb this hill into the face of these descending trucks.

Mac had advised us to lie on the ground, put our ears to a deeply embedded rock, and listen for the vibration, much as we had listened for approaching railroad trains when we were children. He also suggested that we could put an ear to a tree and perhaps hear the trucks. We paid attention to this advice, and it was only after much consultation and repeated "soundings" that we ventured up the hill. The road was so narrow that the jeep's wheels barely fit onto its surface.

About halfway up the hill I saw a sight that I couldn't believe. It was a boy, or so it seemed, coming down the hill toward us, sliding and slipping on the rocky surface. I slowed the jeep to a crawl. There, some fifty yards ahead of us stood the young boy, frozen like a rabbit, startled at the sight of us. I got out of the jeep and called to him. "*Buenos días,*" I said in a soft voice. "*Somos amigos*" ("We are friends"). He turned and acted as if he wanted to run away. I desperately wanted him to stop. I sensed that he needed help, and I didn't want to frighten him. "Would you wait a minute until I can make my jeep climb the hill? I need to ask you something."

"What?" he called back, still poised to run away.

"I need help in finding the next village. Will you wait for us?"

He nodded and started back up the hill. As we came slowly to a halt beside him at the top of the hill, I got a closer look at the thin, bony boy, who looked to be about ten years old. He was dusty all over and had on ragged, torn clothing.

"Where is your home?" I asked him.

"I have no home," he replied, his brown eyes shimmering with unshed tears.

"How is it that you have no home?" I kept my voice gentle. He still looked as if he wanted to run.

"My father was killed, and soon after my mother died of lung disease. My sister went to my grandmother, but there was no place there for me."

"Where do you live then?" I persisted.

"I live in the forest."

It was a chilling statement. I couldn't imagine how this child had survived on his own in the wilderness. I looked at him more closely. He held his head proudly, and intelligence shone from his dark eyes.

"What do you eat, then?" I asked him.

"I know the plants, and I have this." He held up a little bow. "I shoot rabbits and eat them. Sometimes there is work on the road, and I earn a little money."

I was astonished. "How old are you?"

"*Diez y seis,*" he replied. Sixteen years old.

It seemed wrong to let him go back alone into the forest. I don't know when I've felt as compelled to help anyone as I felt toward that young orphan boy. I was furious with the grandmother. How could she let him live on his own when she had any sort of shelter at all?

"Come, ride with us to Nuri. We will eat there, and on the way you can tell me about the birds and plants. All right?"

His eyes shone with excitement. "In the car? You want me to come in your car?"

"Yes. Come with us. Make room for him back there, Jesús, and give him some of those cookies."

"Sure thing, Pat." Jesús made him welcome as we headed toward Nuri.

Although the boy, who told us his name was José García, was shy at first, he told us a bit about himself. After his mother had died, he had gone to live with his grandmother, who had barely enough food for herself and his younger sister. So the boy had voluntarily gone away, telling her he would

find work in the city. She believed him because he always had worked to earn his way as best he could, even when he was a little boy.

As we talked together, José lost his fright, and soon he was proudly showing off his intimate knowledge of the birds and plants of the region. He knew a lot about doves. He told us how he set traps for them and ate them. When he started detailing the medicinal properties of plants of the region, I stopped and took notes.

"Look out for this one," he said, pointing to a scrubby plant with small blue flowers.

"Why is that?" I answered, looking at the plant growing beside the dirt road.

"It is called *mala mujer.*"

"Evil woman?"

"*Sí,* evil woman. The women, they use it when their husbands are mean to them and beat them. No more husband, no more beatings. It is very poisonous."

"I will certainly look out for it." I carefully collected a sample and put it into a bag for cataloging. He showed me the plant from which *manzanilla* tea is gathered, and another plant that is good for fever.

He pointed out kapok and amapa trees growing in great profusion. The amapa trees were in full flower and almost entirely covered some hills with clouds of pink blossoms. The Thorn Forest itself was still brown, making the blossoming trees and plants more beautiful for the contrast.

"Look, *Señor,* the *zopilotes!*" José pointed to a dozen black vultures with whitish undermarkings on their wings. "Something is dead there. They clean it," he said matter-of-factly.

Like most of the mountain people of Sonora, José knew the local names and the uses of most of the plants. It was soon clear that his intelligence was above average. He was astonishingly perceptive and articulate. He had even picked up some English somehow, though he had never been to school. His mounting curiosity and joy at seeing grown men studying nature and his forest was touching, and it broke down the barriers of age and nationality.

The closer we got to Nuri, the more unhappy he looked. He turned to me and said, "*Señor*, will you be coming back to the Sierra? Ever?" His voice faltered as he said the words.

"Yes, José. I will be back, God willing," I replied.

"I'll wait by the road," he said.

I was touched. "José, you can't do that! It will be months before I return. I'm not sure when we'll arrive. We could be delayed."

"It doesn't matter. When you come, I'll be waiting."

José was silent the rest of the way to Nuri. Then I said, hoping to ease his gloom, "José, suppose I write to you from the United States. I'll send the letter to your grandmother's village."

He hung his head. "*Señor*, I cannot read."

"Do you have a friend who can read?"

"*Sí*, my friend Juan—he went to school in Obregón before his mama brought him back to the village. He's the one who taught me English."

"Well, have your friend read the letter, and in the letter I'll try to let you know the exact time when I'm coming. I don't want you to wait for days by the road and be disappointed if I'm not there."

This seemed to satisfy him for a while. Finally we could see Nuri ahead. Then he turned to me, his sad eyes glistening with moisture. When he spoke, his voice was tight with emotion. "*Señor*, please would you take me home with you? I have no father or mother. I will do anything you say. Please take me with you."

In my heart, I wanted to say yes. But my head knew that my family obligations and the immigration laws meant I couldn't. "I don't know that I can, José."

"Please. I'd work for you. You don't have to pay me anything. I'd work very hard."

By this time we were climbing the edge of the escarpment at the outskirts of Nuri, and José was frantic with emotion. "Please . . . please," he pleaded. I felt myself react to his cry for help with such a strong emotion that I could hardly hold back the tears. My hands shook as I held onto the steering wheel.

"José, I don't know how to explain it to you," I said, then turned away from those eyes of his, so naked in their plea.

"Tell me," he said.

"My country has laws about taking people across the border. I wouldn't be allowed to bring you back with me. It isn't possible." The students were silent during this exchange, and it seemed as if this intense young boy and I were alone in the jeep.

"Oh," José said and fell silent. I wondered if I was being honest with him. How could I take home a child—a sixteen-year-old—I had found by the road? What would my wife say? What would my children say? I felt torn by the conflict.

We rode on silently as I tried to understand why this boy had made such a powerful impression on me in such a short time. José seemed relieved when I invited him to join us for supper, and I urged Hectór to bring his guitar so we could have some music.

We went to a small cafe on the plaza and ordered some food. Don found a young American traveler to talk to, a rarity in these parts, and Hectór and Jesús struck up a friendship with some local young people, who formed an impromptu chorus and serenaded the people walking around the square.

After supper José tearfully said good-bye to us and started out alone on foot in the dark of the night over the brown canyon wall. Would I ever see him again? I hoped so. He had tugged at my heartstrings.

I comforted myself with the thought that I had gotten his grandmother's name and could write him. I would try to look him up when I returned. We stayed the night near Nuri, and I went to sleep wondering if I had done the right thing in saying no to José.

From Nuri, we proceeded, trying again to get far enough into the mountains to connect with the Monterde mine. However, our efforts to map a new trail were no more successful than before. The trip seemed to be another failure.

On our way home we stopped again to see Mac and enjoyed a pleasant and interesting visit. Reluctantly we left for Hermosillo. It was a long, tiring, and hot drive. Thoughts of the orphan boy of the Thorn Forest occupied my mind the whole way.

When we dropped off Jesús and Hectór, Jesús thanked me in formal tones, his face sincere. "Señor Jenks, I will come with you again. You write to me and tell me when. It was a great privilege to travel with you."

Hectór had been no less enthusiastic, and I considered our including both of them to be a great success. The car seemed empty without them during the trip from Hermosillo to Tucson.

I pulled the jeep into the street where Don's fraternity house stood. He unloaded his now dusty pack and bedroll and said his good-byes, then walked to his door.

He dropped his baggage, turned, and raised a hand in the air.

"¡*Vamos pa' Yécora!*"("Let's go to Yécora!")

I laughed and drove home to my family. For years to come, Don's expression remained as our standard greeting wherever we met.

CHAPTER 5

A Visit to the Seri

By the spring of 1955, I had traveled to the Yécora area three times since I had met José García. Each time I had looked for him. Each time I had left without finding him.

I was frustrated by my failure to find the orphan boy. No one seemed to have heard of him. It was as if he had vanished without a trace that night when he left us in the square at Nuri.

During those years, Mac and I had corresponded regularly. Each time I had traveled to Yécora, I had brought as much as I could to help him alleviate the poverty of the Pima Indians in the area. Mac's lists had grown so long and the supplies weighed so much that I had had a trailer built so I could carry more desperately needed food and clothing.

Although I continued to search for a way into the mine, I had very little success in finding it. I was beginning to think John Pope would have to find some other way to solve the problem of Doña Poinciana, the woman bandit. By now the mine was in serious trouble financially, and it seemed impossible to reverse the situation by means of a new trail.

But I decided to try once again. I took Don Needham with me as well as Ivan Clark, a young minister from Oklahoma. Eugene Le Fevre, a serious young man who was trying to decide what he wanted to do with his life, accompanied us in another car full of American students, who would come as far as Hermosillo. All of us would spend a day on the beach with the Seri Indians, who live on the Sea of Cortez.

We didn't have much money in those days, and on the way down, we camped overnight in the courtyard of the La Siesta Motel at Hermosillo. The owner was sympathetic to our mission and allowed us to pitch our tents right beside the swimming pool. In the morning we picked up Jesús Lizárraga, Hectór López, and some of their university friends. When I had asked them to join us for a day's visit to the Seri, they looked at me askance, saying, "The Seri? Surely not!"

"Trust me. You'll like it!" I could see from their faces that they had misgivings. But since Jesús and Hectór trusted me, they agreed to come.

It's not that I didn't understand their misgivings. The Seri did not have a great reputation with the other Mexicans and even had been accused of cannibalism. Through the years, an animosity had built between the two groups.

The Seri were fishermen, and when they traveled from their village, Desemboque, to Hermosillo, they rode in the smelly fish trucks. Because of their reputation and the fish smell they carried with them, the Seri were not welcome in stores or hotels. So even when the Seri men did have money,

they slept in the park. While asleep, pranksters took advantage of them and cut off their long, lustrous hair braids, making the Seri men feel angry, humiliated, and embarrassed.

Other Seri men were lured by these same pranksters into the *cantinas* near the park, where the Seri men, who were not used to liquor, got drunk very quickly. Again, off went the braids. For this reason, when the Seri and the Mexicans were together, there was usually a fight.

We bumped along the dirt trail used by the fish trucks until we came to Desemboque. The Seri young people knew we were coming because I had written to some friends who ran a school for the Seri.

As we pulled up, the young Seri came out of their igloo-like huts and stood in a group, their faces sullen. They did not want to play games on the beach with Mexican students. That was clear.

"Come on!" I called out. "We've brought some food and the soccer ball. Let's have a game."

"Go on," the teacher urged. "Pat has come all this way just to spend the day with you."

Staying in a group, the young Seri men walked with us down to the beach. I picked the two teams by splitting up the group of Seri and putting them on teams equally made up of American and Mexican students. I knew if I let them make up a team of their own, there would be a fight as soon as the game was over.

They played a sort of soccer, and soon a wildly spirited game was ranging up and down the length of the beach. As we were playing, a boat containing a Seri fisherman got into trouble. One of the Seri women gave a great wail that sounded like the cry of a gull as the boat was swamped and

sinking. The woman gave the customary cry again and again, sending chills down my spine each time I heard it.

Two Seri men ran for a small boat and quickly rowed to the foundering craft, rescuing the fisherman and towing the boat back to safety. We all felt good to see them walk up onto the beach.

We played until the sun began to set, one of those spectacular and awesome displays of fire and color that only the Sea of Cortez seems to produce. Our group quieted down and came together—companionably by this time—and Hectór got out his guitar. We sang first some songs from the United States, then songs of Mexico, then songs of the Seri, each student making an effort to learn from the others the words to the songs.

As the night grew late, the melodies took on a melancholy air. I think we were all moved by the fellowship between these diverse groups.

All differences seemed to be forgotten now, and the evening ended on a note of perfect harmony. We slept in the schoolhouse that night and planned to return to Hermosillo in the morning. From there, Eugene Le Fevre and the American students would return to the States. The rest of us would travel on, first stopping in Yécora at Mac's to deliver supplies to the Pima, then trying one more time to penetrate the Sierra far enough to reach the mine.

Before Eugene got into his car the next morning, he came to me. "Pat, I know you weren't aware of it, but this experience with you and the other students has made me do some profound thinking. I've been changed by it—in a way that's hard to understand. Thanks for including me in the trip."

"I'm glad you could be with us," I said to him, a little surprised by the intensity of his words. Even so, I understood.

I too felt that something special had happened to all of us as we had watched people turn from enemies into friends and as we had participated in the harmony and fellowship between them.

CHAPTER 6

The Journey to Shangri-la

We traveled back through Hermosillo, where we stopped briefly at the Casa de los Estudiantes to drop off the Mexican students who would not be going into the Sierra with us. Jesús and Hectór would continue on with Don, Ivan Clark, and me. As we got back into the jeep, Don Needham waved an arm. "¡Vamos pa' Yécora!" he shouted at the others, and off we went.

On my earlier trips, I had chosen to travel to Yécora by way of Ciudad Obregón, which meant I had driven 125 miles south to Ciudad Obregón and then backtracked to the north to reach the Yécora area. This time I would try a new route and head straight east toward Nuri. I had been told that the roads were very bad, but I decided to find out for myself. If we could make it, we might save valuable time. If not, we would have to return to Hermosillo and still go south to Esperanza just short of Obregón—losing 200 miles and lots of time.

We proceeded east from Hermosillo until we reached the Yaqui River, and followed it south until we were high above it, on a bluff. Across from us was the little village of LaDura, a dusty pueblo whose inhabitants were connected with the outside world by an ancient, cable-hung plank bridge tied together with rusty bailing wire.

The crossing of this bridge required courage, even on foot, and I hesitated to take the jeep over it. I didn't want to dump a load of young students in the muddy river so far below us. I stopped the jeep and got out.

"I'll walk across it and see what I think," I told the students. "Wait here."

Amused at the wary looks on their faces, I gingerly set out to check the conditions of the bridge. The cables were intact, but rusty. The heavy planks that provided the driving surface were irregularly spaced, and over the length of its 300-foot span there were gaps where four or five boards were missing. These gaps were wide enough that the jeep would have fallen right through. I crossed these spaces by holding onto the upper cable and walking on the cable that supported the boards. I felt quite daring by the time I reached the other side. I had noticed several loose planks that weren't tied onto the cables at all. This gave me an idea, and I returned across the swaying bridge to the students.

"Come with me across to the town. If we can get some more planks, we can fill in some of the worst of the holes."

Jesús gave me an incredulous look. "How will we keep the planks on the bridge?"

"They're only wired on. We'll just fasten them with wire,

then move them along to the next hole. You'll see. It will work."

"Are you sure?" Hectór asked, his eyebrows high.

"I'd better be, I'm driving. Of course if you would all rather drive back to Hermosillo, then another 125 miles south, we could avoid this crossing . . ."

"No, no," they chorused. So we set to work.

We crossed the bridge and went into LaDura, where we found some more planks. I believe what we found were the original planks. The villagers were intrigued by our plan and gathered into a good-sized audience when we put it into effect. Even the old grandmothers came out to watch.

It took a while for us to fill several wide gaps. When we were done, I made the students walk while I drove the jeep alone. I saw no reason to chance more than my own skin to the swaying structure. When the jeep had crossed the first gap I left the vehicle on a solid section, and we all took the planks from behind us and moved them forward to the next gap. Yard-by-yard we made our way across. It wasn't that I felt unsafe. I just felt uneasy as the bridge swayed every time the jeep moved. I was soaking wet with sweat by the time I heard the crunch of gravel under the wheels on the far side. We stored the planks with a villager and paid him a small sum of money to keep them safe for our return.

Now we were on our way to Nuri. As we climbed the hill where I had first seen the orphan boy, José García, I looked for him, as if I really thought I would find him standing by the road. My guilt over rejecting his plea for help had grown in his absence, and now I realized I had almost an obsession about finding him and knowing he had survived in spite of me. I looked for him all the way up the hill, but I saw no one.

As we neared Nuri, we stopped at a little roadside shed

where a man sold soft drinks. The students piled out behind me. All of us were thirsty and tired. I greeted the vendor, and asked him his name. "Aparicio García is my name. Is there anything I can do for you?"

I brightened. "Aparicio García? Would you be related to a young man named José García?"

He shrugged. "There are many José Garcías, so it is possible. Perhaps I am."

I tensed. "This young man lives out in the Thorn Forest. He said his grandmother lived in the village of Guadalupe de la Concepción." I paused, noticing a look of interest on the man's face. I hardly dared hope.

"Of course—José! I am his uncle!" he said.

Excitement surged through me, and my voice shook as I said, "How is he? I've been looking for him for three years."

"It is a miracle, but he is fine. He left the Thorn Forest, and now he lives with his grandmother. He's managed to get some cattle. He takes care of his sister Lupita and his grandmother now. He's a fine boy."

What a sight I must have presented to this stranger— holding back tears of joy and stammering away in broken Spanish, one question after another. The students watched my excitement with astonishment, although I think Jesús and Héctor understood. They had spent the afternoon with José as I had. The orphan boy was alive and well. What a relief! What a joy!

His uncle told me that when José had taken over the responsibility for his sister and his elderly, feeble grandmother, God had provided for them, and they had prospered. Somehow he had accumulated enough money or items to trade to obtain eight head of cattle and one horse. The family harvested wild herbs, fruits from the *papache* shrub, and greens and berries that grew wild in the forest. José got wild game for them, and they had a garden.

My heart was full as I heard these words, and I realized that if I had taken José out of the mountains to come with me, his sister and grandmother would not have had the young man to care for them. I felt better about my decision for the first time in three years. God had cared for this child of the forest and with far greater wisdom than I could have brought to the problem.

The uncle gave us the general direction to the village of Guadalupe de la Concepción, and after I explained the situation to the students, they agreed to make an excursion to the village.

We followed along the road leading from Nuri to the high mountains toward Yécora. We weren't sure of the exact point on the road where the path leading to José's village led away from the road, so we stopped a truck driver.

"*Buenos días, Señor*," I said. "Can you give us directions to the village of Guadalupe de la Concepción?"

His eyebrows rose. His face showed disbelief. "There is no road," he said in Spanish.

"We know, but nonetheless, we want to know the way. Can you tell us?"

"Go down this road to the place where there is a large chimney rock. Look for a trail to the right, through the brush and follow it. You will have to leave your jeep. It's a foot trail."

We thanked him and eagerly followed his directions. I locked up the jeep as best I could and was grateful that I had a newer model with solid covering that was closed up. Even so, I was worried about the supplies. One of the students who was still tired from our night on the beach offered to stay with it, relieving my mind considerably. I didn't want to return and find the jeep gone or stripped.

We made sure our canteens were full of water, prepared ourselves a sandwich, and set off down the trail. We walked for perhaps two hours, at first along a dim footpath that led us over a pass in the mountains and then through some small corn patches into a deep canyon. Here we found a more direct trail that wandered beside a stream in the shade of huge cottonwood trees. Uracas flew over us, filling the air with their harsh cries, their long, blue tail feathers streaming behind them.

The shade felt good, for the day was a hot one, and when a black phoebe flew out of the bushes and ahead of us up the stream, I was delighted. I pointed to the bird and said to the students, "A little bird like that once saved my life."

"How was that?" Hectór López asked.

"I had been exploring the desert with Ernie Serventi, a friend of mine, just south of the border. It was late April, and the weather had gotten hot. We ran out of water, and then we got lost. I was sure of the direction we were heading and knew if we could make it another few hours, we'd run into the railroad track."

Jesús was most interested. "How would that help you?" he asked.

"There are watering stations on the track. One was near the point where I thought we were."

"How did the bird come into it?"

"You know that one of the first effects of dehydration is that you lose your sense of judgment. I've seen people do some really crazy things. Ernie was pretty dehydrated and wouldn't believe my compass was right. He became convinced I was leading us in the wrong direction. He wanted to set off across the sand dunes in the opposite direction from where I knew the railroad had to be. I knew we'd die if we went that way, but he was so disoriented that I couldn't let him go alone."

"How did you stop him?" Don asked. All the students had gathered close.

"Just then a black phoebe flew past us and headed straight toward where I thought the railroad would be. Ernie had spent a lot of time in the desert with me, and both of us knew that the black phoebe lives only where there's plenty of water."

"So did Ernie quit arguing?" Hectór asked.

"Not quite. He was irrational by that time. Finally I told him that the bird had spoken to me and had told me that if we followed him, we would be safe. I cajoled him along, and at the top of a dune, there in the distance I saw a telegraph line and knew we'd found the railroad. We eventually came to the watering station of Gustavo Sotelo. We drank our fill and soaked ourselves from the leading water tank."

"What happened then?" Hectór asked.

"We waited in the shade of the tower. When the train came along, we got on it."

The students and I continued along under the shade of the cottonwoods, and again the black phoebe flashed past. "I do think that's my favorite bird," I said. They nodded in understanding.

On the right side of the stream, the trail branched upward. When we climbed to the top, we had our first glimpse of the valley of the village of Guadalupe de la Concepción. It reminded me of the Shangri-la I had read about.

The village consisted of a tiny collection of small white-washed adobe huts with earth roofs and floors. None of the houses had glass windows, only openings that could be covered with boards in case of bad weather. However, every yard was neatly swept, and each home contained a little fenced garden of flowers and herbs.

I approached a man who was working in a small patch of corn and asked him if he could direct me to the home of José García. He was a fair-haired man with blue eyes, and I thought this odd for a village in the remote regions of the Sierra. He seemed openly curious at our appearance in his quiet village.

He pointed the way, and I thanked him. We headed through the center of the collection of huts; there was no central street. Shy children hid behind their mothers, who stood in the doorways of the little huts and watched our progress. I gave each a friendly greeting, but most of them only nodded. The children vanished immediately behind their mothers' skirts. They were not used to visitors. Many of the women and children were red-haired or blonde, with light eyes.

We came to José's house, where chickens were scratching industriously in the dirt. The dense brush of the Thorn Forest surrounded the village, rising thickly behind José's house. The entire impression of the place was one of neatness and tranquillity.

Pretty soon, a group of older children chattering with excitement gathered round. José came out of the door of his house to see what it was all about. When he saw me, his mouth dropped open in surprise. He ran toward me, arms open wide, and gave me a huge *abrazo*, which I returned, blinking back my tears at seeing him look so healthy. This young man had no idea that he had been a weight on my conscience for three years since I had last seen him.

His face was amazed. "How did you ever find me?" he asked, and I explained about his uncle Aparicio.

"You came all this way to see me?" he asked, over and

over, pleased that I had made such a long trip by foot just to visit him.

"I've been worrying about you! Of course I came to see you. I didn't know you were here until I met your uncle Aparicio, who told me where to find you."

"It is good you did not do as I asked and take me with you," he said to me, his eyes serious. He led me into the hut where his aged grandmother and sister waited shyly. "If I had gone away, who would have cared for them?"

I nodded.

"Now," he said proudly. "You will eat with us?"

I felt alarmed at accepting their hospitality because I had three hungry young men with me, and I knew from experience the sort of appetites they had. But José insisted and explained that they had enough food. His sister, a brown-skinned girl with beautiful eyes and even features, gathered eggs from the chickens and helped her grandmother prepare some tortillas. The grandmother was extremely old, bent over nearly double, her face etched with deep lines. Her body was wrapped in black rags.

None of this dampened her spirits though, and her eyes sparkled with interest. She looked over each of us with great curiosity. Her hair was yellowed from age and the smoke of their cooking fire. She set to work immediately and made us a great stack of fresh corn tortillas, which she served with fried eggs. It tasted delicious, and all of us were grateful for the meal.

After we had talked for a while, José took us to meet his friend and neighbor, Manuel Tineo, an older man with a family and an herb garden. In his garden he grew a plant he called té limón. He picked some and had his wife prepare it for us. We drank it and found it soothing to the throat and stomach. It was so delicious that I asked for a plant to take back to Tucson. Manuel proudly gave me a nice little rooted bunch to plant in my garden. Each time I drink some, I think of that day in José García's village.

We visited for as long as we dared, but I didn't want our student at the jeep to be alone after dark. And we still had to find a place to camp. I finally told José that we must leave.

His face was sad. "I will come with you to the road," he insisted. From the look on his face I knew there was no use in protesting.

"*Muchas gracias,*" I told his grandmother. "You are very kind."

On the way out, I asked José about the villagers, who were almost entirely blonde and green- or blue-eyed. "Why are the people of your village so light?"

"You do not know of the legend of the three soldiers?" he asked me, his face surprised.

"No, I don't think I have heard it."

"It is how the villages began."

"Tell me about it," I said.

"It was a long time ago . . ."

CHAPTER 7

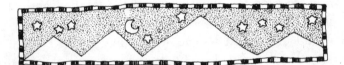

The Legend of the Three Soldiers

"The three soldiers came to our mountains before the middle of the last century, after the United States had invaded Mexico. The first time they came because they were wounded and sick, and our people nursed them back to health. They swore they would never forget us or our kindness to them."

"Who were these three soldiers?"

"You will hear their names all around you, all through the Sierra. They were Clarke, DeMoss, and Moore. After they were well, they went back to their homes in the United States. But the memory of our valley and its people lingered on with them, and so they returned."

"But what did they do here?"

"They came to the village of Guadalupe de la Concepción. They were not the first white men to come. There had been mining here in the days of the *conquistadores*, and a German man had come after the Spanish had been driven away. His children were already here to greet the American soldiers when they returned, and it is from him that many of our villagers get their fair hair."

"Why did I see some red-headed people?"

"Oh, that was from Clarke. He had red hair. DeMoss and Moore were blonde. Anyway, Clarke, DeMoss, and Moore left again."

We had descended to the stream and walked under the trees that lined each side. The day had grown hot, and it was even warm and steamy in the shade of the cottonwood trees.

"So the village was here in 1850 then?"

"Of course." He puffed out his chest. "This is a very old village. Some say it was here before 1635—but I do not know that this is so. I do know that the mine on the hill is at least that old."

"Was it a gold mine?"

"Some gold. Some of the copper and silver bells from the mine are still ringing in other villages nearby."

"So the village has a long history. Why didn't the men stay there?"

"Which men?"

"DeMoss and Moore and Clarke. Why didn't they stay in Guadalupe de la Concepción, where there was another outsider?"

"I don't know, perhaps there was conflict. Anyway, they went and found a place so beautiful they declared it would be their home. They named it after an island they had visited. They called their new home 'Bermudes.'"

"Where is it?" I intended to visit this place. I was getting more and more interested in these remote villages. It seemed the people who lived in them had something different, isolated as they were from the rest of the world.

"It is near Yécora. Do you know Yécora?"

"Yes, we're going there now. I'll ask about it then."

"Anyway, the soldiers settled in Bermudes, and their children had children, and soon the whole valley was full of blonde and red-haired children. When you go there today, you will find the names of the people are Clarke and DeMoss and Moore. They all have the blonde hair and green eyes or red hair and blue eyes. They are very beautiful people, especially the women." He said this somewhat wistfully.

I stumbled on a protruding root and young José shot out an arm and affectionately steadied me. "*Cuidado, Señor,*" he said.

"Thank you. So none of the people in your village are descended from them?"

"Some perhaps. Indeed, who knows? We call the light ones *perlas*—but they may be the children of the German who came and married one of the women who was already there."

"What was his name?"

"I don't know. He took the name of his wife, perhaps so he could own part of the mine. He became very wealthy but he never left our valley. He had nine daughters and three sons, and it is from them that the light ones come."

"How did you come to live there, José?"

"My grandmama and grandfather were born there, and my parents too."

"You mentioned the day I first met you that your father died. How did he die?"

His face darkened. "There are many widows in the hills,

and my mother was one of them. My father was shot in a feud."

"And your mother was ill, isn't that right?"

"Yes. It was a very bad winter. Many died." His eyes were sorrowful.

"So there's another side to this Shangri-la," I said in a soft voice.

"What?"

"Nothing."

We walked on for some time in silence, and soon we were climbing the steep, narrow trail back to the road. The higher we climbed, the more distressed José became. He didn't want us to leave. Finally, we climbed out of the trees. The student we had left with the jeep was delighted to see us, and there were greetings all around.

I turned to José to bid him good-bye. "I'll be back to visit you again, José," I said to him.

"Do you promise?"

"I promise. I'll come back."

"I believe you." His face brightened. "After all, didn't you come and find me in my village?"

We piled into the jeep, and now I was eager to be on our way. José stood beside the road, and I watched him grow small in my rearview mirror. We reached a bend in the road, and I turned for a last look and waved to him. Then he was lost to sight behind the high hill.

We continued on to Yécora, and there Mac confirmed the story of the three soldiers who had come to the valley in the high Sierra and stayed. As was often the case in our travels in the Sierra, by the time we had finished delivering the supplies to Mac, it was time to go home again. I left feeling unsatisfied, as if I had had only a small taste of a delicious dish and wanted more but couldn't have it. I vowed that on the next trip I would seek out the other villages of the valley that I now called Shangri-la.

Still, I consoled myself that while we were distributing the supplies we had brought in the little trailer, I had met one of the DeMoss descendants and had been most impressed by him. He had invited me to visit him on my next trip. That day began a long friendship with José María DeMoss.

That night we had a good visit with Mac, and once again I was impressed with this recluse from the modern world. Mac regaled us with stories of his adventures in the Sierra. I was intrigued by one of them, which told about a treasure he himself had hidden in an old mine shaft. I hoped he would allow me to help in its recovery.

It had taken us longer than we had thought to distribute the supplies, and the students needed to get back for their classes.

We rose early in the morning and departed in as much haste as we could muster in the early-morning darkness, loading the jeep by lantern. Then everyone piled in. I drove as fast as I dared on the rough roads and bounced myself and my young passengers considerably. Fortunately, they were good natured about it. Their youthful resilience and high spirits brought zest and joy to our adventures.

At one point I found a relatively smooth *arroyo* going in the right direction and used it for a road. The locals called it Arroyo Reparo. I could see from the occasional clumps of manure that horses had been this way recently.

We followed it as it sloped gradually downward, and soon I grew confident and increased my speed. We careened around a clump of bushes, and there, in the shade of the bushes, we surprised a man and a horse. The man seemed to be a Yaqui Indian. When we lurched by him, we saw a look of outrage on his face, apparently because we had caught him with his faded jeans down around his ankles as he squatted on the sand to answer the call of nature. His horse had been standing quietly by, waiting for his master, until the roar of our jeep startled him and caused him to bolt into the dense brush that grew next to the wash.

The man leaped to his feet, his pants still around his ankles. I didn't stop the jeep to apologize, as I should have done, because I really didn't want a confrontation with him. In my rearview mirror I saw him raise his right arm, make a fist, and shake it at me three times.

The rest of the trip to Tucson took three full days. I thought no more of the man we had so unkindly disturbed.

Some days later, I received a phone call from Travis Edmondson, a good friend who lived in Tucson. He had spent some years living with the Yaqui people who were grateful to him for his advice to them during a crisis when many Yaqui lives had been saved. Over the years he had become their trusted friend and advisor.

"What did you do in Mexico?" he asked me.

"What do you mean?" I responded, amazed that he even knew of my trip.

"I've gotten a message by Yaqui heliograph that you have offended their headman. He wanted to know if they should kill you."

"What?" I asked, astonished. I knew about the Yaqui heliograph. I had seen it working, using the flashes of sun from the mirrors of the signalers on the top of peaks. I knew it was a fast and accurate method of sending messages and that word of my coming had often been flashed ahead of my actual arrival.

"Pat, this was serious. If I hadn't intervened for you, you could have been killed."

"Killed? Good grief." Then I remembered. "I think I know what you're talking about."

"What on earth did you do?"

"I spooked a horse, and I guess I should have stopped to help the man get it back, but I was in too much of a hurry."

"I told them to leave you alone, that you're a good man and a friend of mine. But be careful! They take an insult very seriously."

"Thanks for the help, Travis. I'll be careful. Do you think I should find the man and apologize now?"

"No. I'll apologize for you. But watch it."

"I will. Thanks again, Travis."

I hung up the phone, shaken. The Yaqui's trusted relationship with my friend had saved my life and the lives of my students. I had no doubt of it. Travis's call was a friendly one, but its message was not.

I was a stranger in the Sierra, and I must take care not to offend again.

The next time I might not be so lucky.

CHAPTER 8

The Feud

"Pat, this is John Pope. I'm afraid I have some bad news for you."

I gripped the telephone tighter. "What is it?" I asked, although I suspected I knew.

"You may as well quit trying to find a trail in from the west to the Monterde mine."

"What's happened?"

"I'm afraid we've lost it. We've had to close down. We weren't making enough even to pay salaries anymore. I've found a buyer in Mexico, although I feel sorry for him if he thinks he's smarter or tougher than Doña Poinciana."

"I can't say I'm too surprised. Thanks, John, for calling me to tell me yourself."

"It's the least I could do. I know you've really tried to find a new way for us to ship, but I realized that it was a long shot when I asked you to do it. I hope you understood that and don't feel you're in any way personally to blame."

"No, I know that I'm not. Still, I wish it had worked out. If it had, I would have been able to get my doctorate in ornithology."

"I'm really sorry. I did everything I could think of. Doña Poinciana has the area so tightly under control there was just no way to get past her."

"Well, we tried. Of course you know me well enough to be sure that I was having a good time in looking for a new trail. I've met some wonderful people down there."

"I hear some of them haven't been so wonderful."

"That's true." I laughed, thinking of some of the problems I had had. "On the whole, it's been very enjoyable. What are your plans now, John?"

"I've been offered a teaching position at a university in Mexico City, and I've decided to accept it. I'm looking forward to living in a city after those years in the mountains."

"The best of luck to you. Be sure to keep in touch!"

"Of course. Good-bye, Pat. Sorry it couldn't have worked out better. I know you could have used the money, but I did the best I could."

"I know that, John. Good-bye."

I hung up the phone and turned to Julia. "Did you hear enough to know what's happened?"

She nodded. "The mine has gone under. Now you can spend your time in Mexico larking about instead of hunting for a trail and not finding it. I'm sure it will help you be in a better mood after you return from a trip to Mexico."

I smiled a little sheepishly. Julia had always had me figured out. She knew I loved to explore and camp under the stars and that I probably would find a way to do it somehow, even without a legitimate purpose.

"I'm disappointed that the mine has gone under. That was a big investment."

"Your father knew it was risky when he did it. It was a long shot that didn't work out."

The closing of the mine didn't end my travels to the Sierra. It only gave me greater freedom to visit the many friends I had made and to further explore the area.

In the fall of 1955, I made a trip to La Coja to visit the ranch of David DeMoss, whose name was handed down from the original David DeMoss—one of the three soldiers José García had told us about. I rode the lead horse along the narrow mountain trail. I had taken Jesús Lizárraga and Gilberto Fierro with me. Gilberto, a dark-haired, dark-eyed young artist, was so talented it was difficult to believe he had never had an art lesson. He carried a sketch pad with him wherever he went.

We rode down the trail toward David DeMoss's ranch in good spirits, singing, talking, sometimes riding quietly. It was during the quiet times that I thought about what Mac had told us about the DeMoss family feud. Three years ago, a dispute about a seven-acre plot of land apparently had broken out between Enrique DeMoss and his uncle Francisco. One night after drinking too much, the two men had had a serious argument and Francisco rode away. The next day, from a distance of 300 yards, Enrique had shot his uncle through the heart with a 30/30 rifle. Even though the *cordado* soldiers had come and taken Enrique away to the federal prison, Francisco's widow and nine children had not been satisfied, and a feud had sprung up between Francisco's family and Enrique's.

Adding to the pain of the situation was the manner in

which Enrique had been taken away. When a man is arrested by the *cordado,* his thumbs are wrapped in wet leather, and he is strung by them with long leather cords to a horse ridden by the official from the government and forced to walk the long distance to the prison behind the horse. If the man falls, he is dragged until someone notices he has fallen; even then he is not helped to his feet. He must continue on as best he can. If he attempts to escape, he is shot.

Seeing their father taken off like that had only reinforced the feud for Enrique's children. For three years, the hostility between the two groups had steadily increased to the point that any spark would set off more killing.

We were on our way to see David DeMoss, Francisco's son. As we climbed through the pine forests toward the grassy mesa and the La Coja ranch, we were approached by two riders. We greeted them warmly, but instead of the usual friendly hello and exchange of conversation we were used to, the young men—boys, really—rode on without even glancing at us or acknowledging our existence. We were shocked and worried by this—even more worried to see that each of the boys carried a rifle on the saddle of his horse.

"I think Mac was right," I said to Jesús. "I'm really worried about this."

We arrived at the ranch of David DeMoss and were greeted warmly by Mrs. DeMoss and two of David's sons, José María and David, Jr., whom everyone called Suni. As soon as I had the opportunity, I took David aside and asked him about the young men on the trail. "Such anger," I said to him. "Please tell me about it."

His face flushed red. "It does not concern you," he said. "It is a family matter."

"I am concerned, my friend. I will pray about it."

As I left the room, Mrs. DeMoss stopped me. She had

been waiting by the door. "Please help us, *Señor* Jenks. I fear one of my sons will die next. It is very bad, this feud."

I opened my mouth to reply, but she was gone, her face pale with anxiety.

No more was said of the matter that night. We shared the wonderful meal Mrs. DeMoss prepared for us and went to our beds. I lay awake much of that night, prayerfully seeking a solution to the situation that I knew was endangering the lives of my friends. I was acquainted by now with the mountain people, and I believed Mrs. DeMoss was right.

By morning, in answer to my prayers, I was led to believe that I ought to try to end the feud between the two branches of the DeMoss family. I spoke to David once again and asked if I could present to him and his family a proposal to end the feud.

"It will do no good," he said, his face hard, his jaw set.

"Please, let me try. Let's pray about it together. The feud is not good for either of your families. One of your sons will be killed if it keeps on."

"All right. We will pray with you."

The DeMoss family believed that if a candle was lit when prayers were said, the prayers were rendered more effective. We gathered round the table in the kitchen of the log house. With great solemnity, David lit a candle and placed it on the table. Then we joined hands and bowed our heads. With the greatest sincerity I prayed that Enrique's family would receive me in their home and listen to my prayer for peace.

When we had finished, David said to me, "Pat, we worry about this. They might kill you before you can tell them why you have come."

"Don't worry about it. I'll be fine." Inside I was wondering, but I kept my words brave.

We talked about it, and I agreed that I would go down the

hill from David's home and up the trail to the other side, to the house where Enrique's children were now living and running his portion of the ranch. Enrique's widow had gone into Bermudes to live. The ranch and its memories were too painful for her.

I set out at once, down the rocky trail, crossing the little stream on the stepping-stones used by the two families as a bridge for at least a hundred years. I saw no sign of Enrique's family as I climbed toward their house, a sturdy structure built of logs.

I remember that climb well. I knew I was being watched, for the DeMosses, both friend and enemy, have eyes like eagles. As my feet crunched on the gravel of the path, I could feel those eyes watching me. My mouth grew dry, my skin prickled. There was not a sound from a human, no cry either of warning or of welcome, and I knew that behind me all the area held its breath. My friends had warned me that to cross into the valley of their enemy was surely to risk my life. I began to doubt myself, and my steps slowed. But I had come this far. I determined I would go on and do the best I could.

Taking a deep breath, I went up to the door of the house and knocked on it. Still no sign of life. I felt my heart pounding in my chest. Should I give up? A red-tailed hawk screamed behind me, startling me, its distinctive, harsh cry echoing over the hills. I knocked again.

The door opened slowly, and I stood face-to-face with the head of the enemy clan. My heart was in my throat, and in that moment as I looked at his surly face, I wondered at my sanity. This man's father had killed my friend's father. How could my efforts, no matter how well-intentioned, end that? We stood and looked at each other, the tension almost palpable between us.

I almost bolted and ran but decided against it. I had

prayed, and this peace initiative was what I had been led toward. So I forced a smile onto my face, cleared my throat, and explained in my faulty Spanish why I had come. I could see his brothers, children, and wife inside the dimly lit room behind him, their faces unsmiling, frightened.

"Come in," my host said. His eyes showed suspicion and fear, and I saw that I was off to a bad start.

"I came to talk with you . . . about the feud," I said. Looking around and seeing only hostility in their faces, I went on trying to explain the reason for my coming, handicapped by my lack of precise words to express the message I had brought. Gradually, their innate kindness and courtesy toward strangers won out, and I realized they were helping me with my Spanish, helping me to explain this mission of peace.

"We prayed and lit a candle," I said. This impressed them. The lighting of a candle has great power among them, and I could see the faces relax. Hope and curiosity crept into the green eyes around me. "The family across the canyon wants to end this feud, to bury it as if it had never been, never to mention it or its cause as long as all shall live." I stopped here and stayed silent for a long moment while they thought about it.

"How could this be done?" the headman asked.

"Let me pray with you. I will pray that there be peace again with you, so your children can feel that they can ride without weapons, so they can be smiling again, so you can laugh and be free again of this terrible tension. Three years is long enough!" The room seemed filled with emotion, and there were tears in the eyes of the women.

"Let us discuss this among ourselves," the man said. He took the family out into the kitchen, where I could hear voices raised and heated discussion going on. I hardly dared to hope. Finally, after what seemed to be a long delay, the family came back in, and I saw by the shy smiles of the little girls that I might have reason to rejoice.

"How do you think this feud can end?" the man said to me.

"First, let's pray together, and we will also light a candle," I answered, my voice shaking a little from emotion. "Then I will go to the family across the valley, and tell them that we have agreed that both of your families will meet at the stream, and together we will pray again, and we will all light candles. At that point each will embrace, and the feud will be ended. It will be as if it never happened."

"Agreed!" he said to me, and with a heart full of joy, we solemnly lit a candle, and I led the family in prayer. I then made an agreement with them that I would talk to David's family. And if all was still well and if they agreed to meet at the stream, I would go out on the promontory and raise my right hand. When they agreed, I shook hands all around and left the cabin.

My feet flew as I raced down the hill, across the stream, and up the other side. I could see David and his family waiting in a group beside the big tree at the top of the hill. Their postures revealed their stress. When I was close enough for them to see my smile and wave of the hand, they relaxed and were chattering excitedly when I got close enough to tell them what had happened.

"It's going to be all right," I said. "They have agreed to meet with you."

"Where?"

"In the middle of the stream," I answered.

Mrs. DeMoss smiled widely and gave me a warm hug. "*Gracias, Señor* Pat. You are a good man," she said to me, then hurried off toward the kitchen.

After explaining the details of my conversation across the valley to David DeMoss, he agreed to the process I had worked out. His eyes were moist with tears by the time I had finished, and I knew he was greatly relieved to be done with the feud. But all wasn't finished yet.

"I must go out and signal to them," I said.

They watched as I went out to the promontory and raised my right hand, holding it in the air for a very long time, my heart full of joy at the success of the mission.

This time I could see the other family out in the open, in front of their house. I prayed a prayer of thankfulness and asked God to stay with us through the actual meeting, about which I was still quite nervous.

We then gathered the family together, not forgetting some candles to light together. I kept a smile on my face in an attempt to hide my anxiety over the meeting.

We went to the lip of the trail above the stream and looked across to the other family, who unsmilingly looked back at us. I led the way down, and the others followed. The only sounds were our feet on the path and excited breathing, betraying the apprehension we all shared.

We met at the middle of the stream. I reached out both arms and pulled the patriarch of each family toward me, enclosing them both in an embrace. This broke the tension, and soon all members of both the families were hugging each other, and laughter and excited talk filled the air.

On a more solemn note, I led prayers for peace and happiness and reminded them that this was the last time there would be a mention by any of them of the feud between them, or its cause, in their families. We lit the candles, all of us. Our prayers were over, and so was the feud.

We all returned to David's home, where his wife had prepared a wonderful meal in large quantities. As I prayed before we ate, my heart was full of joy at danger averted and prayers answered. It was a truly happy occasion, and the families enjoyed a meal together for the first time in three years.

CHAPTER 9

Suni

My friend Gordon McMurray often wrote to let me know of some family in dire need in Yécora, and I would load my trailer with food and other necessities that my friends would donate for the needy family. I came to enjoy Mac's company so much that seeing him again was reason enough to make the drive. But I also made new friends.

In the spring of 1956, I traveled once again to the Sierra, taking with me Don Needham from Tucson as well as Jesús Lizárraga and Fausto Penunuri, both from Hermosillo. We traveled to Yécora to spend some time with Mac. As we sat talking, a young man came into the room. He looked familiar to me, but I didn't recognize him until he spoke. When I heard his bell-like voice, I knew he was David DeMoss, Jr., or Suni, as people called him to distinguish him from his father. As he joined in the conversation, I was impressed by the good manners and thoughtful comments of this seventeen-year-old.

When we left Mac's house, we went to La Coja ranch, the DeMoss family home, where Suni's family lived. I saw again the deep *barrancas* in this valley of the Sierra Madre. Mrs. DeMoss, who had become very fond of me after I helped to resolve the feud, fed me great quantities of roast chicken, tortillas, and the delicately flavored squash she grew in her garden. Her round face was flushed from cooking the meal on her large wood stove. With sparkling eyes she watched me eat everything on the plate.

After the meal, I sat outside in the midst of the flowers and enjoyed the view of the mountains. An acorn woodpecker searched for insects under the bark of the oak tree near the back door, and the mourning doves filled the air with their soothing call. It was a peaceful setting.

"*Señor* Jenks?" I heard. It was Suni, approaching me with a shy smile on his face.

"Here, sit beside me," I said to him.

"*Señor* Jenks, when you leave here, could I come with you as far as Nogales? I have never traveled outside of the valley, and I would like to see what there is to see . . ." His voice trailed off, and he looked down at the ground, as if suddenly embarrassed at his own boldness.

"I'll ask your parents, Suni. If they agree, I'd love to take you with us." I was delighted that Suni had brought up the subject, and I immediately went to David DeMoss to ask if Suni might come along with us partway. He agreed readily.

Because we had planned to return that afternoon to Yécora, we hurried to pack some things for Suni and saddled up our horses. We rode from La Coja to Mesa del Fraijo, where I had left the jeep. When we arrived, Emilio Fraijo's wife had a wonderful meal waiting for us, and after emotional good-byes, we set out.

I eagerly looked forward to showing Suni the wonders of civilization. Suni was delighted to ride in the jeep—his first experience in any sort of vehicle.

"Come on, Suni, sit in front," Fausto encouraged.

"Yeah. You're in for a treat on the road to Nuri, and you need to have a good view," Don said with a grin.

"Don't worry. Pat's driven it before," Jesús said, giving Suni a reassuring pat on the shoulder. Jesús, as always, was sensitive to the feelings of others.

As we bounced along the road, Fausto began the singing, and from Mesa del Fraijo to Tezopaco, where we left Fausto and his music behind, the car rang with the sound of one song after another. I loved this, and it always made our journeys fly by.

I wanted to show Suni cities and civilization. I intended to show him as much of Guaymas and the towns on the way to the border as I could.

"What are you doing?" he asked.

"That's the gearshift. I'm changing the gears to match the need for power." A blank look came on his face, but I could see from his round eyes that he was most impressed by the noise I made when I didn't shift quite as smoothly as I should have.

We were a happy group as we continued on, but as always, it was a hot and dusty ride. By the time we reached the Sea of Cortez, south of Guaymas, our clothes stuck to our sweaty skin, and the dust of the road coated every inch of our bodies.

We saw a sign that said "Cochori Beach," and we turned

toward it without hesitation. When we reached the ocean, we piled out of the car, which had become like a sauna. We kicked around a soccer ball until we got to the water and then ran into it to cool off. As soon as Suni hit the water, he came out crying, sobbing really, and I thought perhaps he had stepped on a stingray and been hurt.

I hurried over to him. "What is it, Suni? What's wrong?"

He was crying so hard he couldn't answer, and I put an arm around him and led him away from the water. As far as I could tell, he didn't seem injured.

"It's the water—it's turned sour." He looked at me with great sadness in his eyes, and I realized he didn't know the sea was naturally salty.

I tried to reassure him. "It's all right, Suni. It's supposed to be that way. You don't have to drink it."

"No, Señor Jenks, you do not understand. The water, it has turned bad. All of that water is spoiled."

"It's the ocean, and that's how the ocean is, Suni. It's not bad water."

Now he looked stubborn. "The water is supposed to be sweet. I know it because on our ranches we take the water from the streams and it is sweet. Go and taste it, Señor Jenks. It has turned bad—the whole thing. It has all gone bad." He waved an arm toward the sea, and his handsome face was deeply distressed. Tears still streamed down his cheeks.

I felt a pang in my stomach. What could I do to calm him down? Then, far off I saw a dark shape in the water. "Suni, look! Way over there!" I handed him my binoculars and pointed offshore to a school of dolphins cavorting. He watched until the dolphins submerged, then turned to me, his eyes wide with wonder.

"Fish can live in the sour water?" he asked in amazement.

"Here, come over with me to the water's edge." He

followed me obediently. "See those little bubbles in the sand? Now watch."

I squatted down on the sand and dug quickly, turning up a clam. "Creatures live in the salt water—millions of them. It's not spoiled water. It's just salty."

His face was relieved. "I'm so glad. That is too much water to waste."

"You can't drink it, Suni. It's too salty, so we still need the water from the streams. But this is how the ocean is supposed to be."

Satisfied, he went back to join the others. As he waded back into the ocean, I could see him eyeing the water with suspicion and putting a taste of it to his lips.

We had a lively soccer game after our swim and then went on to the Malena Restaurant. I loved the Malena's food and ate there whenever I had the chance. It was cool inside, with bright *serapes* decorating the walls. We took seats at two small formica-covered tables, pushing them together so we could all sit together.

"What are those?" Suni asked, pointing to the lights.

"Electric lights, Suni. These are how we see at night in the city."

"What is *eléctrica?*" he asked, for I had used the Spanish word.

"It's a sort of . . . uh . . . current that flows through wires, like water flows through a pipe."

"What is a pipe?"

I looked to the other students for help. They stayed quiet, but their faces were amused at my predicament. "A pipe is like the hollowed logs that bring the water to the tank by the kitchen at the home of your friends, the Coronados."

"Oh, they have such a thing here?" he asked, diverted at the thought of finding something familiar.

"Something like that."

"But how does the light flow through a pipe into a tank? I do not understand."

"It's a sort of invisible thing." From the look on his face, I knew I wasn't convincing him of anything. He waited for me to tell him about this miracle. The other students were openly grinning now.

"Boys, help me out here. I'm trying to explain to Suni what electricity is." Jesús tried to explain, but he had no better luck.

We had a moment of reprieve as the waiter came and took our food orders. We ordered an immediate round of Cokes. It had been a thirsty ride. When the Cokes arrived, Suni drank his right down, then looked around the room again.

"What is that?" Suni asked, pointing to the fan, seeming to give up on the question of electricity.

"It's a fan," I responded.

"What makes it go round and round?"

My heart sank as I answered. "Electricity."

"¿Eléctrica?" Disbelief again. "No, Pat. You told me that was what made the lights work. How could it make the fan work while it is making the lights work?"

I tried my best to explain, without success. I looked up to see the waiter bringing steaming plates of Mexican food to the tables and naïvely thought the subject was closed.

"Where did the food come from?" Suni asked.

"The kitchen," I answered.

"What kitchen? Food cooks on fires." Here certainty showed on his face. In his house a fire cooked food, and that he knew to be a fact.

"In this kitchen, they have an electric stove," I explained.

"Ha! This is not so. Food cooks on fires." He began to eat his lunch, a look of pleasure on his face.

After lunch we went to my friend Manuel Mercado's house, where we picked up Manuel and his guitar before setting out for the harbor. We were excited to find several big cargo vessels docked there. I had been able to get tours for my students on cargo vessels like these before and was hopeful that I could do so again.

We spotted a huge, new-looking German ship, which I decided would be a good one. I went up the gangway and asked for the first mate. When he came, I told him we had a boy who had never been on a ship and would like to see theirs. The first mate welcomed us aboard and told us he would show us some of its gadgets. One of the English-speaking sailors took us into the radio room and showed us the kind of radio telephone into which you speak and your own voice plays back to you at the touch of a button. He demonstrated it and asked if one of us would like to try it.

"Let Suni do it. This is all new to him," I said.

Suni talked obediently into the microphone. The sailor then pushed the playback button, and Suni's voice filled the little room.

Poor Suni! His jaw dropped and his face went white. He dropped the phone and bolted from the room in a real state of panic. Too late I realized that he thought it was a spirit talking to him and was very frightened.

We all ran after him, but as we burst from the door after a bit of a jam-up, all of us trying to get out at the same time, we saw Suni running toward the rail. My heart dropped. I thought he would leap over it.

A quick-thinking sailor saved him by grabbing his legs. I ran to Suni and apologized for scaring him.

"I'm so sorry you were frightened, Suni. I didn't realize you wouldn't understand." I sat beside him on a crate until he calmed down. We were joined by the ship's crew and spent a pleasant hour visiting together, with Manuel strumming on the guitar. Then the first mate gave us a tour of the ship.

That night we camped on Miramar beach and had a wonderful evening of song. The next day we proceeded north to Hermosillo, where we left Jesús Lizárraga at the Casa de los Estudiantes. We would take Suni all the way to Nogales with us, and I hoped to be able to take him across the border for an ice-cream sundae at a place called Zula's. The border guard at first was hesitant to allow Suni across the border, but I finally convinced the guard that I was an honorable man and would have Suni back before his shift was over.

We went to Zula's and had hamburgers and ice-cream sundaes—delectable concoctions piled unusually high with whipped cream and nuts with a big cherry on the top. Suni loved his sundae, and after he finished it, he asked for another. I ordered another one gladly and enjoyed watching him eat it.

"*Señor* Jenks, may I have another?" he asked me politely.

"Of course," I replied. "Only one more, though. If you eat more than three, it upsets the stomach."

"I understand. This is the most delicious thing I've ever tasted."

We watched in awe as he finished his third sundae. Then came a sad time, for we had to take Suni back to the border. Don and I wanted him to have a souvenir of our trip, so we outfitted him with all of our spare clothes. At that time the Mexican government had a regulation that you could return with only the clothes you could wear. We sent Suni back with three pairs of socks, two pairs of trousers, three shirts, a sweater, a jacket, and two hats—he was wearing them all. I crossed the border with him and took him to the bus station.

"Good-bye, Suni. I have a present for you." I handed him a New Testament in which I had written in the frontispiece.

This little gift goes along with my admiration for you. You have shown the spirit of Christ within you. In being willing to forget the past troubles [here I referred to the feud], you are one of my greatest and most important friends in the whole world. God will remember you for this. This little book contains the secrets of a happy and successful life. Read it carefully and slowly, and leave yourself enough time to think about it. I will be happy when I see you again, and we can talk about some of the precious ideas contained in this book.

My regards to your father and to all of your family.

From your good friend,
Randolph Jenks

Suni accepted the book gratefully. "Good-bye Pat, and thank you for showing me the city."

"You're welcome. Someday I would like to take you to my ranch. Then you can stay for a long visit. Okay?"

"Okay."

I talked to the bus driver and made sure he would see that Suni got off at Esperanza, where he would ride in a friend's lumber truck back to Yécora. He would have to walk from there to La Coja ranch.

Don and I stood and waited for the bus to pull out and take Suni back toward his beautiful mountains. I felt sad that I wasn't going with him. I realized that the Sierra had gotten a strong hold on me.

CHAPTER 10

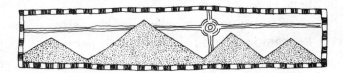

The Wedding Trousseau

In the winter of 1956, on a return trip from Yécora, we took two young men from the high valleys back to our ranch in Tucson. One of the young men was nineteen-year-old José María DeMoss, son of David DeMoss. José was a handsome guy, with bright and smiling hazel eyes, and thick chestnut brows that nearly came together when he frowned. When he worried, his nose became wrinkled like a corrugated washboard.

José María's name was a traditional one, the name always given to the firstborn son or grandson. The name related back to Christ's father, Joseph. Literally, José María was named after Joseph and Mary.

José was an intelligent person who expressed himself with sincerity and honesty. We studied birds together, finding some mountain trogons, spotted screech owls and pigmy owls, as well as several rare parrots in the hills surrounding his home. He showed a keen interest in my books with pictures of birds and mammals. Whenever we had gone hunting on his father's ranch, José displayed an uncanny ability to put himself in the position of the hunted. He literally never came back empty-handed and was the envy of his brothers and cousins.

The second young man was José's cousin, Leobardo Clarke. Leobardo was a direct contrast in personality to José María and was so shy that it was hard to get him to talk at all in English. We had gotten along well on several trips into the mountains beyond the Clarkes' ranch in Tezopaco. I looked forward to returning hospitality to both of these young men, whose families had so warmly shared with me their home and life.

Both young men displayed curiosity about what we saw as we passed through the bustling cities on the way back to Tucson. Their innate dignity and good manners allowed them to fit in anywhere I took them.

We stopped first at my home in Tucson, where they impressed my wife with their good manners and my children with their skill at the lariat. While we were in Tucson, I introduced them to a little of city life. We went to a movie—their first—and a symphony concert.

Later I took them out to the ranch, about thirty miles away, and started them on the project they had come to help me with—the fencing of some range. They worked on the ranch during the week and spent the weekends with my family in Tucson. José María's English improved each day. Leobardo, on the other hand, wouldn't venture a word in

English, which limited his communication with people at the ranch and at my home.

When I had taken the young men across the Mexican-U.S. border, I was able to get a permanent visa only for José. Leobardo was allowed only two months. When Leobardo's visa neared its expiration, I tried to extend it, but it was refused. We had to take him back to Nogales and put him on the bus, where he would proceed as far as he could, then take a lumber truck to his village.

In the meantime, José María had begun the process of fitting in with all of us, and we enjoyed him immensely. Every night he sat at the kitchen table and wrote letters to his family. He missed them and was very sentimental and open about this. His tenderness endeared him further to us. Some of his letters were apparently to a young woman. We were surprised one day when he came to us, a letter in his hand, and announced, "I am to be married."

Julia and I looked at him and congratulated him. "That's wonderful!"

"You will please help me with something?" he said to me.

"Well, of course. What is it?" I answered, thinking he wanted some fatherly advice.

"I must buy my bride's clothes."

"Oh, no," Julia said, a little shocked, I think. "The bride buys her own clothes."

He looked down at the floor for a moment, then said, "In my country, Señora Jenks, the groom, he buys the wedding dress."

"Oh, I didn't realize that. I was thinking of our customs." Julia then tactfully withdrew to the other room while I stayed with my young friend, whose skin was now a bright shade of red and whose nose was wrinkling and unwrinkling from his tension. It was clear that the whole subject was embarrassing to him.

"*Señor*, it is not only the dress I must buy. I'm so ashamed," he said to me. "I must buy everything." Here he waved his hands vaguely in the area of his chest and grew even redder.

"Everything?"

"Everything. I must buy it all. Will you help me?"

"Well, of course, I'll help you, but don't you think it would be better if Mrs. Jenks went with you?"

"Oh no, I couldn't . . ." Here he began to stammer, and I realized it had taken great courage for him to admit to me that he must buy undergarments for his bride-to-be. It would surely be impossible for him to confide this to my wife, even though she was an understanding woman and he seemed fond of her. I hated to admit it to José María, but I had never shopped for such things myself and was a little embarrassed at the idea of it. When I started to try to tell him this, I looked at his face, and the expression on it was so desperate, I knew I would have to help him. I was a little amused in spite of myself. So much for my image of myself as a man of the world.

"All right, José María, we'll go into Myerson's White House department store on Saturday. The owner is a friend of mine, and I'm sure he can get someone to help us."

He beamed at me. "Thank you, *muchas gracias!*" He then fled the room.

I went into Julia's room. "Julia, he wants me to help him buy the bloomers and all for his young lady."

She had a good laugh at my expense and wished me the best of luck. During the next few days I would catch her with an odd little smile on her face, and I knew she was thinking of my errand on Saturday. The truth of it is, I had never paid much attention to women's clothing, and it would be a case of the blind leading the blind. Every time I thought of it, my gloom increased.

Finally, in fact all too soon, it was Saturday, and we set out bravely. I had resolved to treat it as just another shopping trip. We matter-of-factly asked Hymie Myerson for his help, and he assigned a pretty young woman to assist us.

José María was so embarrassed that he wouldn't face her, and she had the unfortunate job of talking to a young man who mumbled and stammered and who finally faced into the corner away from her. She turned to me for help, and my face went as hot and red as José María's had done in our home.

"He needs to have a complete wedding outfit. Everything for the young lady," I said, biting the bullet.

"Everything?" Her eyebrow crooked up, and a little smile twitched at the corner of her mouth.

"All of it."

"You mean the dress, the shoes, and the veil?" she asked, her face all innocent, her eyes wide, that little smile still twitching. The woman was a sadist.

"And the other things as well."

"Other things?" The smile was twitching at both sides of her mouth now, and her eyes held a distinct gleam of amusement.

"You know, the bloomers and the brazier?" (Here I used the word for a charcoal cooker, but I honestly think I had never said the word out loud before.)

Now I think she took pity on me. "Oh, of course, I understand. Come over to this counter. We'll start with the underthings."

At this José María buried himself further into the corner. A pile of coats nearly hid him from view. I stood in front of a counter where various things with straps and lace were displayed. I tried not to look at them.

"Now what size does the young lady wear?"

"Size?" I said, panic seizing me. "I don't know what size. How would I know the size? I've never seen the young woman."

"I must know the size. Obviously, women are shaped . . . uh . . . differently in this area." She motioned toward her own chest. "She could be shaped small . . . or large."

"Oh dear. Let me try to find out." I went over to José María. He was so shocked at the topic he even turned from me and would not speak at all. He was now the color of a beet. I returned to the saleswoman in despair.

"Pretend you're shopping for yourself," I said. "Make everything in the size you wear."

She seemed a little offended at this, and I stumbled around a bit before hitting on another way to put it. "No, I don't mean pretend it's your wedding. I mean pretend the woman is your size. Then we'll buy everything as if she were." I was pleased at this. It seemed as if it would be the solution to the problem.

Even so, the woman insisted on showing me things and spread out an assortment of brassieres for me to make a choice. I pointed blindly at one, as two women shopping nearby watched me with what I considered an impolite degree of interest.

We then moved over to the counter where the bloomers were displayed, and a similar scene followed. José María still hid in the corner, trying to make himself disappear.

Sweating now from the stress of it, I picked out a slip. Then we moved on to wedding dresses. I asked for something in a reasonable price range, and she brought a dress that looked as if it had been around for a while, but the lace

looked nice, so I bought it. I began to feel better. The worst was over. My friend Hymie found us an old traveling bag that had been in the window too long, and I packed away all the items.

Now I felt relieved. My duty was accomplished. José María and I had a soda at Walgreen's and proudly took the things home, where I couldn't wait to show Julia how well I had done.

Soon after, José María left Tucson and headed south, taking the bus as far as Esperanza. From there he would ride a lumber truck to Mesa del Campanero and Mesa del Fraijo, where he would deliver the trousseau to his bride, then walk across the mountains to La Coja ranch.

Julia was too nice to tell me what I had done, but about a month later she asked me about José's bride-to-be. "What size is she, Pat?"

"Oh, I think she's quite small, according to José María. About the size of Marie" (one of our daughters).

"It will be interesting to see the dress." Something about her tone alarmed me, and I turned to see a smile on her face.

"Why? What's wrong with it?"

Amusement twinkled in her eyes. "Marie is a size 10. The dress you picked was a size 40. That's quite a lot too big. I thought the bride must be a big girl."

My heart sank.

"Another thing," Julia said, not done with me yet.

"What, dear?" I answered, not really wanting to hear it.

"The underthings were all different sizes, some of them quite small and some of them quite large. I don't know how they could fit the same woman."

I had a vision of the bride, arrayed in this unlikely assortment of clothes and remembered that some of the things had looked a little big, especially the dress. Guilt swept over me, and I was quiet for a long time.

Julia patted my hand. "Don't worry dear. Maybe the bride knows how to sew."

In my imagination I replayed the scene of the bride rejecting poor José María and tossing the clothes I had picked out into the street after him.

CHAPTER 11

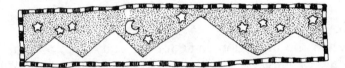

A Mountain Wedding

We didn't hear much from José for a while. Then one day we got a letter inviting us to his wedding. Apparently the bride hadn't rejected him after all.

In the spring of 1957, Julia and I traveled to the Mesa del Campanero and José María's wedding. Once we got to the rough roads, Julia clutched the sides of the jeep so hard her knuckles were white for hours at a time. I had told her the road was a bad one, but words could never adequately describe how bad.

I think my relaxed manner at the wheel caused her even more anxiety, but nothing could dampen my enthusiasm for at last showing my wife the high Sierra and having her share with me the adventure of getting there and meeting the people who had become my friends. The weather had cooperated, and the spectacular scenery showed itself to full advantage. I rejoiced at our finally being able to make the trip together.

I share with you Julia's account of José María's wedding, for I find her eye for detail on the event to be better and more interesting than my own.

◆ ◆

When the invitation came for Pat and me to attend José María's wedding, my reaction was a womanly one. What should I wear? My second reaction was to José's request that Pat and I be the best man and matron of honor. We were delighted at that and made our plans with excitement. I hadn't been into the Sierra Madre with Pat but was happy at the chance finally to do so. I was eager to see what it was that drew him there several times a year, year after year. I share Pat's love of the outdoors and had prepared for the trip with great anticipation.

We were on the road—*road* is a charitable word—and I can only say that it was a horrendous drive. We came to the listening hill, where you must listen to the rocks and trees. It was just as Pat had told me, dangerous and narrow, with the edge of the road crumbling off into sheer precipices to the side. What he hadn't told me and what I didn't expect was that this stretch of road would last for hours and hours. The entire climb had to be made in compound gear because of the steep grade. The car made a horrible noise, as if it would grind itself up all the way to the top. When we finally came off the road and arrived at the mesa where our hosts, the

Coronados, had their house, I was aching from the jolting and in great need of a bathroom.

The Coronados' house, a well-built log structure surrounded by lovely flowers, was a welcome sight. Several members of the household were working in the garden as we drove up, and wide smiles came to their faces when they saw us. José María had arranged for us to stay with them, so we were expected. The sons of this family were very tall and quite handsome; they stood to greet us as we brought our dusty vehicle to a stop.

We were greeted with great enthusiasm and given an *abrazo* by each member of the household. Mrs. Coronado, understanding that I might need to relieve myself, took me to a secluded area behind the house, around behind a great tree. She explained in Spanish that this was the women's tree and pointed to another large tree in the opposite direction, the men's tree. My Spanish was not too good, but I did understand her meaning.

Afterward, she escorted me to a nice room with a Sonoran cot covered by a beautiful embroidered sheet. It was exquisite work. Pat and I had brought our sleeping bags and put them inside. I think the cot was too narrow for both of us in any event, but our hostess was distressed to think we were more comfortable in our bedrolls than on the cot.

Mrs. Coronado then showed me the rest of the house. She was a little shy but quite proud of their home. In the kitchen she showed me her huge, cast-iron, wood-burning stove and introduced me to her tiny Pima maid, at whose skirts clung two small Pima boys, her sons, I think.

There were children in the Coronado household as well, but they were huge in contrast to the Pima children. A little fight came up between Sergio, a Coronado son, and one of the Pima boys. It seemed it was all right for Sergio to beat up the little Pima boy, but the Pima wasn't to strike back or he was in dreadful trouble. This upset me, but I was a guest in the house and said nothing.

This poor treatment of the Pima was explained by Mrs. Coronado's comments to the census taker, who came along shortly after we arrived. She carefully listed for him all of the members of her household and even described us as two guests visiting from America. She neglected to mention the Pima family, who lived in a little shack away from the main house. When I asked her about this, she looked at me in amazement. "We don't count the Pima, ever!" It was clear she had not even thought about it before.

The house had running water from a tank, an ingenious arrangement built by Mr. Coronado, who had been very upset that the women wouldn't let him pipe the water right into the kitchen. A little way off they had a well equipped with a hand pump, with which they filled a tank. From this tank, the water ran downhill into another tank called a *pila*, located just outside the kitchen door. The piping was cleverly made of hollowed-out logs. From the *pila* the women brought the water into the kitchen in buckets. They were quite happy with this arrangement and had a strong prejudice against running water in the house.

We had arrived on a Tuesday, and later that day one of the children fell and got a small cut on his leg. The child was wailing pitifully, and I prepared to dress the cut with the medical kit Pat always carried in the jeep. But when the child's mother saw what I was doing, she snatched her child away from me. "You don't treat the sick on Tuesday!" she told me in shocked tones.

"You can't be serious!" I responded, aghast.

"It is forbidden."

Pat came up just then and quickly explained to me that it

was an absolute taboo, so strong that if a woman went into labor on Tuesday, no one would help her, or if a man was shot on Tuesday, no one could tend his wounds. I started to question this, but Pat shot me a look of warning, so I backed off. Pat told me later that he had never been able to figure out the source of this taboo.

I also learned that after childbirth neither the mother nor the newborn could be cleansed for three days. To me this might have some foundation in the need to protect the two against the chilly winters. I could sympathize. I had been cold since we arrived. Although it was mid-afternoon, I was wearing my sweater, coat, gloves, and cap. I was still cold.

Later the Coronados served a wonderful meal on a table set beautifully with fine, thin china with a delicate pattern of violets. The meal was some sort of tasty meat, vegetables, tortillas, beans, and a dessert of *flan*, which is a delicious custard with a caramel topping. After the meal we sat around and visited for a long time. Then Pat pointed across the valley to the little village of Mesa del Fraijo and asked me if I wanted to walk there or drive.

"Oh, let's walk!" I said, eager for some exercise after my meal. Besides, it didn't look far.

"Good," Pat agreed. He liked to walk and would enjoy showing me the countryside at a slower pace than that allowed by the jeep. So we set out. Soon I was puffing and panting in the high, thin mountain air.

What I hadn't realized was that distances are deceiving in the mountains. It was one mile down to the valley from the Coronados' house and another mile on a trail that ran nearly straight up the side of the steep hill to the little village that was to be the scene of the wedding. By the time we arrived, I had shed my coat, hat, and gloves.

The village itself was like something from a picture book I

had read as a child. It had a fairy-tale quality, and I could see why Pat had spoken of this valley as Shangri-la. The village was charming, with little log huts evenly spaced along a wide avenue. And lining the street were blossoming fruit trees— pear and apple mainly, but there were a few apricot and peach trees as well.

Each house had a neat log fence, a yard full of brilliant flowers, and a carefully tended garden. The houses were made entirely out of logs, as the Coronados' house had been. The windows had no glass but were closed by a neat arrangement of shutters when the weather was bad. Most of the people we saw were fair skinned and had light hair and eyes. We surmised they were descended from the DeMoss, Clarke, and Moore families.

We went to the house of the bride, whose name was María Osorio. She had been expecting us and was dressed in a pink linen dress I had sent to her. I could see immediately that the dress had been much too large for her. She was a tiny person, scarcely bigger than the Coronados' Pima maid. Nonetheless, María had apparently taken apart the dress and reassembled it in a cut-down version. She had done it so perfectly that I couldn't tell the difference from the garment as it had looked when it was new. She looked beautiful. I smiled to imagine how she had felt when she had seen the size 40 wedding dress, which would have covered two or three of her.

"Welcome, *Señor* Jenks and *Señora* Jenks," she greeted us, a shy smile on her face and courteous dignity in her manner. She took us into the room where the wedding cake stood, ready for the festivities the next day. It was a magnificent cake and looked as if it had been prepared by the fanciest bakery.

"I made it myself. Do you like it?" she said, her eyes modestly downcast.

"It's absolutely beautiful. You have great talent!" I said to her, impressed by the whole situation.

Only two pieces of furniture stood in the room. One was the table that held the wedding cake. The other was a trunk, filled and overflowing with fine embroidered items. I supposed it was a kind of hope chest and contained items for the bride's new home. The delicate handwork on the linens was so fine that the front could not be distinguished from the back. It reminded me of the Appalachian region of the States where needlework is actively practiced as an art in the midst of rough surroundings.

Then we went outdoors to meet the bride's family, who were engaged in building a split-log platform for the dancing that would follow the wedding. A canopy was erected over the platform, but the cover had not yet been made. I wondered what it would look like.

Then we were taken for a visit to every family in the village. As I recall there were nine or ten houses, including that of the bride, and the ritual was the same at each. First we were introduced and warmly greeted by the owners. In half the houses, the family was headed by a woman left a widow by family feuds. It was a sad thing.

Even so, there was nothing sad about the greetings we received. In each house we were invited in and fed. Always we felt compelled to eat, or we knew we would have greatly offended the hostess. We were given tea and something like bread or tortillas. I remember in one house, the charming woman and her daughter served delicious hot rolls with a center pocket that contained a generous spot of jelly. I enjoyed these very much, but by the time we had made the rounds of all the houses, I was extraordinarily full, and I confessed to Pat that I didn't think I could make the walk back across the valley. I stayed at a house in the village while he walked back to get the jeep. He returned about an hour later and parked the jeep outside the village.

We said our good-byes and in one of the houses, which belonged to another branch of the Coronado family, the hostess wanted us to stay the night with her, not with our hosts across the valley. She took me into the bedroom to show me where we would sleep, and there was a fine four-poster bed with beautifully embroidered, encrusted pillow covers and cover sheet—far too nice to sleep on.

We declined firmly but politely and said we must be on our way. The wedding was to be that night, and I was determined to have a nap. We drove back across the mesa and explained to Mrs. Coronado that I would like to rest. "I'll wake you up before the wedding. Don't worry. It's a good thing you will have some rest first."

I lay down and had a good sleep, tired from the walk across the valley in the high mountain air and from the huge quantity of food we had eaten.

Mrs. Coronado, true to her word, wakened us in time to dress. She then fed us some very strong herb tea, which she said would help us to stay awake through the night to come.

I dressed for the ceremony in a nice dress and jacket, but I was so cold that I covered it up with my sweater and coat and then put on a woolly cap and gloves. I felt a little embarrassed to be so bundled up; the cold didn't seem to affect our hosts at all. I climbed into the jeep beside Pat, and we drove across the mesa to the wedding, about a three-mile drive across the canyon.

I learned that my duties as matron of honor were typical ones, with the added duty of dressing the hair of the bride's sisters, who had beautiful, long brown hair. I thoroughly enjoyed this part of my responsibilities.

The wedding was to take place at seven o'clock, and I

hurried, not wanting to delay things. To my surprise, as seven o'clock neared and the sisters' hair was nearly finished, no one made the slightest move to get the bride ready.

Time passed, and it neared eight o'clock. María, who would come to our ranch in Arizona after the honeymoon, got a Sears catalog out of a drawer and began looking at pictures of refrigerators. She asked me to show her what the refrigerator would be like in the home on the ranch to which she and José María would eventually come. I tried to indicate to her what sort of appliances were in the kitchen of the little house that was to be theirs and wondered whether the wedding depended on my answers, for the house was furnished with appliances that were small and old.

She eventually put the catalog away and began brushing her own hair. It was clear that none of them expected anything to happen soon. I went outside, alarmed at the turn things were taking. "Pat, what on earth is going on?"

He looked worried. "I don't know. Mac got here a little while ago. I'll go ask him. Maybe he'll know." Off he went, and after an animated discussion among the men, he returned.

"Well, a problem is holding up things," he said. "It is the custom that three sober men must be present as witnesses at the wedding. The problem is, there don't seem to be three sober men in the whole village, so the wives are going to work to sober up three of the men. When that's done and it's clear that the men are sober, the wedding can take place."

The wedding party seemed to take this all in stride. To relieve the waiting, someone started up with a guitar and another one joined in. Soon the little village rang with music. During our nap, a canopy of fresh evergreens had been put above the dance floor, and the air smelled of pine and wood smoke. A fiddler joined the little band, and I enjoyed the sound of it. Again it reminded me of Appalachia.

At last it was time for the wedding, and I went to help the bride with her gown. As she dressed, she explained, "I wanted a priest for the marriage, and it makes me sad that this isn't a religious wedding."

"Why couldn't you have the priest, María?"

"I did ask for him, but he told us that for him to come so far would be a big expense. There was not so much money in the whole family, so we have the justice of the peace."

As she put on her gown and the beautiful veil that went with it, I was amazed. In the same expert manner that she had altered the pink dress, she had altered the wedding gown. She must have taken it entirely apart and put it together again. It looked absolutely perfect, complete with a long train. She wore a triple strand of pearls and long white gloves, although the sleeves of the gown were long lace. She had delicate, white satin slippers and carried both a Bible and a bouquet of flowers.

I carried her train and worried about it because the floors of the log cabins were of packed earth, and each room was separated by quite a high log threshold. I helped her through the rough doors without a problem and into the living room, where the justice of the peace sat at a table and everyone else stood up. By candlelight the bride's father gave her away, and she and José María were united in marriage. It was a tender moment, and I felt privileged to have shared it.

As soon as the wedding was over, a receiving line was formed, and as best man and matron of honor, Pat and I took our places. Here occurred the most charming custom. As a man greeted one of the women in the line, he placed his left arm on her right shoulder, and she took his right hand in a handshake, then both dipped at the knees, the woman in a little curtsy and the man in a bow. The entire assemblage greeted each member of the receiving line in this manner, and it was like a carefully choreographed dance as the line bobbed up and down.

Finally, after all the guests had been greeted, we ate and drank from the ample supply. Then the wildest sort of music began to play, and the dancing began under the canopy. It was nearly two o'clock in the morning now, and even with our naps, Pat and I were quite tired. Pat sneaked away and asked José María when they would cut the wedding cake. José María answered in astonishment, "Not until the wedding breakfast, of course!"

Pat and I had a hasty conference and decided to slip away for a few hours of rest, then return for the cutting of the cake at the wedding breakfast. We did this and returned in time, thanks to the travel alarm clock we had brought with us. To our delight, as we neared the scene again in the early hours of the morning, the dancing was as wild as it had been when we had left it, and the line of widows still surrounded the dance platform, their feet keeping eager time to the music.

Finally the sun's rays pierced the horizon, and the cake was cut. Coffee, scrambled eggs, and beans were served. Soon after this, the bride and groom climbed into a truck and drove off. No sooner had they gotten the truck into the proper gear, than every man present pulled out his pistol and began to shoot. At this point, the men were far from sober, and the shots went in every direction.

Terrified, I plastered myself against the side of the house, hoping to be out of the line of fire. Soon Pat appeared beside me. We clung there for a long time as this pistol salute to the bride and groom went on. Finally, when it died down, we ventured forth timidly, expecting to see bodies littering the ground.

None were there, and we were relieved to see that Mac also had survived the celebration. The guests mounted their horses and galloped off through the pine forest over the mesa or into the hills. Soon the bride's family were the only ones there, and we said our good-byes and thanked them for the wonderful experience and for having invited us.

At this point, María's family insisted that we take all the rest of the food with us. We declined, not wanting to deprive them, but the bride's mother insisted. So we set off with a huge piece of the wedding cake and plenty of supplies for our trip home.

We stopped at Reparo, where a man with a peg leg was the owner of the only house. He lived there with his daughter. The man invited us to eat with him, but I was a little apprehensive. Pat had once told me that on one of his earlier trips, the fellow had been out of food and had cut the hide off a burro carcass, sliced it into strips, and cooked it for them.

This trip, though, "Peg-leg," as he was nicknamed, gladly agreed to share some wedding cake with us. We had cake and coffee and quite a nice visit. As we drove away, I was thankful he was out of burro hide.

The group at Mac's house; Mac at left. Next to him are Pat Jenks and Benito, Mac's adopted orphan.

Antonio Davila, the artist Gilberto Fierro, and Francisco Ulloa.

At LaCoja ranch; David DeMoss and Leobardo Clark serenade the guests.

The group at LaCoja, where the fued was settled—all faces smiling.

Jesús Lizárraga with some lady friends.

Mac with his orphaned Pima, Benito Juarez.

Benito

Pat and Mac

Fausto Penunuri of Tezopaco.

Fausto doing a traditional Yaqui dance

The group at the Coronado ranch

Young Pancho (Panchito) Duarte of Yecora, October 25, 1958. Sketch
by Gilberto Fierro (see page 160).

Pobre Manuel, as drawn by Gilberto Fierro, October 27, 1958.

Federico DeMoss, drawn by Gilberto.

Sketch by Gilberto, May 15, 1958.

CHAPTER 12

Proving the Inner Light

I'm a man who tries to live by Christian principles. During all of my trips to Mexico, I have not been shy of sharing this viewpoint with the students who accompany me. I had noticed that although we had our share of adventures and hardships, the young men responded favorably to our trips and seemed to gain confidence and faith because of them.

I had been taught and I believe that the light of Christ is present in everyone, even people who have committed crimes and who think about nothing but their own pleasures. I wondered if taking such a person along on one of our trips would result in bringing out that light the way it had been brought out of the other young people who traveled with me.

One summer I spent a lot of time in the area of a cabin I owned on Mount Lemmon, up in the pine forest of the Santa Catalina mountains north of Tucson. I had been clearing hiking and horseback trails all through the forest and had built some redwood boxes to collect cool water and provide drinks for thirsty hikers. I had put a hook and tin cup on a chain at each of these water stations so that everyone could drink.

Some young men from an Air Force radar station at the top of the mountain had discovered me at my work, and soon a couple of them regularly joined me. As we chopped away at the underbrush together, I told John, a young sergeant, of my wish to expose a real bad apple (for that's the way I put it) to one of our trips to Mexico.

John said he knew just the fellow. Although the man he referred to was an Air Force medic in a responsible job, he had gotten into all sorts of trouble, even to the point of being court-martialed twice. The medic's rank had been reduced as a result of this.

"Could you arrange for me to meet this man?" I asked.

"Are you sure you want to? This guy is very nearly a criminal. He doesn't have any friends. He's lucky he's not behind bars."

"He sounds perfect!" I responded. And so the experiment began. That afternoon we drove into town, and I brought my slides of last year's adventures among the Pimas. John went and got the man, and we watched the slides together.

To John's astonishment, but not to mine, George Nolan, the young medic, said, "I'd give my right arm to go along on a trip like that."

"What can you do?" I asked him.

"I'm a medic," George answered. "I can take care of all

sorts of medical needs, even surgery if the problem isn't too difficult."

"Can you take along a complete medical-supply kit with everything you'll need?"

"Sure. No problem. I can get everything."

I wondered whether he would get it legally, but said nothing and waited for the day of our departure with anticipation. All the way into the Sierra, George was full of bragging tales of behavior that to me seemed scandalous. He couldn't speak five words without two of them being cusswords.

"Come on, George. Pipe down. Pat doesn't like that kind of talk," Don Needham said to him, giving him a light punch on the arm.

I could see George's face in my rearview mirror. "What do you mean?" he said, his face astonished.

"Cussing. He doesn't like it."

"Cussing? Oh." He was quiet for a long while, and I wondered whether I had made a mistake to bring him along. Then George began to talk to Don, and when we picked up Jesús Lizárraga and Fausto Penunuri at Hermosillo, George was enthusiastic about learning some Spanish. Fausto was terrific with his guitar and taught George a couple of songs on the long ride into Yécora.

As we came down the road toward Mac's house, an Indian came out to the road in a state of great excitement. We stopped and tried to talk with him, but he seemed to be deaf and mute. Even so, he tried to communicate with us by means of pantomime. He leaped into the air, then fell down on the ground as if he were dead.

We didn't understand, so he did it again, this time flapping his arms like a bird before falling prostrate into the dust. I became alarmed at this point, sure that something had gone wrong at Mac's.

My wife's brother, Bill Swan, had mentioned that he and a friend of his, Ike Russell, might try to fly into Yécora and land on the meadow. I had a terrible feeling that something had happened to their plane. As we neared Mac's house, I looked in disbelief at Ike's airplane, which had crashed and demolished the front porch of a mountain cabin.

From the state of the wreck, I feared the worst. My mouth was dry with fear as I stepped on the gas and sped the rest of the way to the house. There was no sign of anyone near the wreckage.

I stopped in a cloud of dust, and almost immediately Bill came out of Mac's front door. To my relief, he was fine. But his companion, Ike, had a bandage around his head to hold his jaw in place, and he had lost many teeth. He seemed to be in great pain.

When I asked Ike about it, he answered, "Hey, Pat, don't worry about it. I'm glad to be alive."

"But surely you need a doctor! Do you want George to look at it? He's a medic."

"That would be good."

George looked at Ike's jaw and said he thought it was broken. He gave Ike some pain medicine and said, "Get home as soon as you can. I think you need to see an orthopedic specialist for this. It's more than I know how to deal with." I was reassured by George's recommendation. I had worried a bit about the brash young man stepping past the limits of his medical knowledge.

"We'll ride out on the lumber truck tomorrow. Will you bring out the engine for us?" Bill asked.

"How will I get it out of the wreck?"

"Use a hatchet and chop it out. It's broken free of the

engine mounts anyhow. It's worth a good bit of money, even after the crash, so I'd appreciate it if you'd bring it home with you."

"All right. The trailer will be empty anyway."

We went inside Mac's house and set up our cots. I had warned the students about the fleas, and when Mac left the room, we treated the room with some spray I had brought. I don't know if Mac noticed that our visits seemed to drive the fleas away. If he did, he never mentioned it.

We had planned to start treating the Indians the next morning, but I had forgotten the Tuesday taboo. We had a day of leisure instead.

Mac loaned us some horses, and the five of us set out for the hills above Yécora. George was interested in medicinal plants, so I showed him the torote, a small dry-looking tree that had scaling, peeling bark.

"You make a tea of this to help the kidneys. It's reputed to be very beneficial."

George took a piece of the bark and put it in his pocket. "What's that tree?" he asked, pointing to an evergreen oak with large, thick, flat leaves.

"It's a cusi. Those others are cypress, and of course those are the pines that are the target of the timber companies."

He looked around. "This is really nice country. I like it. Thanks for bringing me with you."

"We had better have some lunch and get back to Mac's. I want to get the tents set up."

On our way back to Yécora, we passed several small bands of Pima Indians on their way to get medical treatment. Mac had kept his promise and sent word out to them.

On Wednesday morning, a long line of Indians of every age and description waited for us to begin. We said good-bye to Bill and Ike and set to work.

As I looked at the worn faces of the older Indians and the hopeful eyes of the young ones, I prayed that our skill and supplies would do some good. I need not have worried.

George was a born medic and took over his mission with all the bedside manner of a doctor. He radiated confidence. He patted the patients reassuringly on the back and examined them as if he had been born to do it.

I recall one little girl with a horrible leg wound, perhaps from barbed wire, that had festered and was full of maggots. I had seen a lot in my life, but when that child took off the dirty rag that covered the wound, I had to turn my head away. The other Indians pressed close to George as he performed his examinations, and a murmur of excitement ran through the group as they watched to see what he would do. With Jesús translating, George began a gentle conversation with the little girl.

"It's a terrible wound," he said.

She nodded shyly and agreed.

"In order to make it well, I must cut away the bad part. . . ." Here the little girl looked frightened and shrank back against her mother, who had brought her to our medical camp.

In an understanding and sympathetic tone, George said, "I'll try not to hurt you, but if it does hurt, I want you to give a big yell and cry as loud as you want. All right?"

She nodded. "Now, may I clean this wound for you and make your leg well?" He waited respectfully for an answer from this brown-eyed girl, and we all held our breath.

"Sí, Señor, clean it," she finally said. She stuck out her tiny jaw, and I prayed that her pain would not be too great.

Here the actor in George showed up a little. He set out a table and covered it with a sheet of clean white paper. He took out his instruments and some medicines. The circle of

watching Pimas followed his every move. That little girl's surgery was definitely a big production, and I think by George's actions the child felt honor-bound to endure the thing and proud to have the attention of this important American.

Finally George was ready. He helped the child up onto the table with tenderness and some reassuring words. His face was serious as he began, and the camp grew totally silent except for his murmurs and comments.

"Here, Pat, hold this. I need you to pour alcohol over my hands." I held the bottle and did as he asked. To the Pimas it must have seemed almost like a religious ritual.

"I have some novocaine, and that should help." He prepared the injections and numbed the leg. The little girl looked frightened but resigned. I moved over to stand next to her and held her hand, praying all the while.

At this point George took up a scalpel. Its sharp blade glittered in the sun, and the crowd gave a hiss as all inhaled in unison. As the scalpel touched the wound, a drop of blood appeared. The silence was so complete I heard the birds in the forest a good distance away. George had a little sheen of sweat on his forehead, and I knew then that a lot of his act was bravado. I hoped his skill was as real as he had boasted it was.

The knife moved quickly now, and as he opened the wound, a great gush of pus spurted out of it, the stench so bad I had to turn my head. George didn't waver but pressed the knife gently into the rotting flesh, cutting away everything infected, making a clean edge. He washed the wound with some water he had boiled earlier and carefully cleansed the terrible hole. He had some sulfa powder ready and dusted the wound carefully. There was very little bleeding.

The girl never winced through all of this. She didn't utter

a sound. Instead, she looked at George's face with complete trust.

George then sewed the wound closed with tiny stitches, perfectly spaced. I was filled with admiration—and, in a way, pleasure—that the thing was working out so well. When the wound was closed, George gave the mother some medicines for the little girl, who had been running a high fever because of the infection. He couldn't find a dressing big enough to wrap the leg properly, but Fausto offered his soft white undershirt. It first had to be boiled to make it sterile. The little girl had to wait beside the clinic most of that day while the shirt dried. Finally, George was able to bandage the wounded leg.

The girl left the camp after much praise from all of us for her bravery. She was to come back each day for a checkup, and we waited anxiously for her return, hoping that George's work would hold up.

Most of the people came to see us because they had terrible sores on their bodies. A lot of these were facial sores, and George treated each of them with ointment after cleaning them of dead tissue. He was gentle, and I especially liked the way he reassuringly patted each patient on the back when he was finished.

Jesús and Fausto helped with the eye-infection cases. Many of the people had terrible infections, much like "pink eye." Each of these people had to come back every day for applications of ointment to their eyes, and the pink-eye line was a long one each morning and evening. In this we could help out, and I was proud to see that by the time we left, an entire group of people had been cleared of eye infection for the first time in years. Even that small thing contributed to their comfort, and I told George how grateful I was to him for this.

The day's work done, we would all relax and go back to Mac's house, where we would have supper. Each night we shared a simple meal of meat, tortillas, and beans. We spent the evening together in good conversation and singing with Mexican young people in front of the fire. It was a good feeling I had, seeing the healing my young friend had done each day.

George's fame as a healer spread, and during each of the remaining days of our visit, more and more Pima Indians were in the lines for help. The young girl with the leg wound was at the head of the line each day, and it was gratifying to see the healing process take place on her tiny leg.

We did the best we could for each of them, but all too soon it was time to pack up the camp and start for home. On the last day, I was standing next to George when the girl came in for her checkup.

"How is the leg?" George asked her.

"Much better. See?" She took the bandage off and smiled shyly at him as she showed him that the cut was almost completely healed, although there was an ugly purple line where George had stitched it together. He snipped the stitches and pulled them out.

"You were a good patient," he said, smiling at her, a look of tender pride on his face. I felt tears sting my eyes as I realized how profound the changes had been in the attitude of the young man. His defensive bravado was gone, and in its place was a new seriousness of purpose. His cussing hadn't vanished, but it seemed that the steam had gone out of it. I watched as the rest of the patients went past him.

The pink-eye patients came to show us their clear eyes and told us they could see, "even as we arise in the morning," referring to the fact that before George had arrived, their eyes were always stuck shut when they awakened.

"Mac, I'm leaving you the rest of the eye ointment," George said. "There's no need for them to suffer so much from infection. I'll send you more with Pat when he comes back. Just put it in their eyes for five days in a row, and the infections should clear up."

"Thanks, George. That will save some eyes."

"In fact, let me leave the whole medical kit with you. Maybe you can do some good with it. Also, I brought down this book." George rummaged in his bag and brought out a medical text and handed it to Mac.

"This will help a lot. Thank you," Mac said.

As we began taking down the equipment and stowing it in the jeep, an old Pima woman came up to the makeshift clinic, hobbling as if she could hardly bear to walk. Many Pimas had arthritis, and it seemed likely this was her problem. As she approached, her face twisted with pain, I wished somehow I could ease her distress. She began talking to Jesús, who translated for George. "She's coming because of her rheumatism, and she would appreciate it if we knew how to cure it for her," he said to George.

"I have some aspirin, but that's about all I can do for her," George said.

The old woman went on, talking animatedly to Jesús, who responded to her comments respectfully, then turned to us to translate. "She also says she wants to thank us for relieving the suffering of her people. She says she will remember us forever."

I was pleased at this comment, and as she continued in Spanish along the same lines, I grew a little embarrassed. I tried to respond to her courteously in Spanish, to thank her for her kindness. As so often happens with me when I try to speak Spanish, I couldn't think of the right words. I knew how to say "*Muchas gracias por su . . .*" which meant "Thank you for your . . . ," but the words for "kindly remarks" just wouldn't come. *Aha!* I thought, *"Things of the mind."* And the word *mentiras* came popping into my head.

Pleased with myself, I said to her in a sincere tone, *"Muchas gracias por su mentiras."*

"Oh!" she said, that response apparently meaning the same in Spanish and in English. The smile left her face in an instant, and her face froze. She lifted her chin, and her eyes flashed. Then her body, crippled and bent over only moments before, straightened up as she wheeled about, as if she had never suffered from rheumatism in her life, and she stalked away.

I heard a shout of laughter and turned around to see Jesús and Fausto doubled over.

"What did I say?" I asked Jesús. I knew by this time it wasn't what I had intended to say.

"You told her . . ." He was laughing too hard to talk. The old woman continued her indignant march away from us, her back stiff and straight with fury.

"Tell me what I said to her."

"You thanked her for her lies."

"Oh, no!" I exclaimed. "Go after her and explain for me that I only meant to thank her for her kind thoughts." Jesús ran after her and a spirited discussion followed between them.

He returned to me and said, "It's no use. You aren't forgiven."

"I'm really sorry about that," I said.

"I wouldn't worry if I were you," he responded. "You cured her rheumatism. She hasn't walked so well in years." He grinned as he said it, and I turned to finish packing up the camp.

I had promised Bill Swan that I would haul out the engine

from the wrecked airplane, and that took up a good part of the afternoon. Finally, we were ready. We had just enough time for a walk in the hills before supper.

"Have you been to visit José Juan yet?" I asked George.

"Who is José Juan?"

"The mummy of Yécora."

"Of course I haven't. I've been in the clinic every day."

"Let's go there, and on the way I'll tell you about him."

CHAPTER 13

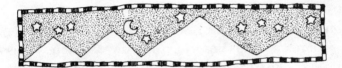

The Mummy of Yécora

The hill was near Mac's house. George and I set off on foot.

"Have you heard of the oracle of Delphi?" I asked George.

"You mean the Greek legend?"

"Yes. Well, the mummy is sort of the Yécora version of the oracle. The Pimas call him José Juan."

As we approached the trail leading up to the cave that was José Juan's home, I saw that we were to have a demonstration of the mummy's role. On the trail were some Pima Indians, down on their hands and knees, creeping up to the entrance. We followed closely behind them, but they ignored us.

"Sh-h," I said to George. "Listen to what they're saying."

"¡José Juan!" called out one of the Indians.

We listened but could hear only the wind in answer.

"¡José Juan!" the Indian called out again, and we heard the Indians in excited conversation from the trail some twenty yards above us. The Indians crawled through the opening and vanished into the cave. We followed close behind them and crouched just outside. George positioned himself so he could see into the cave. We heard one say, "Is it time to plant our crops yet?"

"Feel his hair," another one said. "That's how he will tell you the answer."

One of the Indians crept forward and reached up a hand to the mummy's head. José Juan's body was fully preserved, propped against the cave wall, his knees at his chin in a classic burial posture. A shock of fine, dark hair still adorned the mummy's head, and it was this that the Indian touched.

"It is not curly," he told the others.

"Then it is not yet time to plant the corn," the leader of the group pronounced. "Leave him some food. We will come again when the moon is new and ask him then."

The Indians left bowls of corn and tortillas and backed out of the cave, nearly bumping into us. As they straightened up on the trail, I asked, "Did he talk to you this time?"

"Yes," the leader answered. "He told us it is not yet time to plant our crops."

"How will you know?"

"When his hair is curly in my hand, I will know he has answered us and that it is time to plant."

We said good-bye, and I took George inside the cave to see the mummy, which had acted as an oracle for the Pimas for as long as any living Pima Indian could remember. George wasn't comfortable with José Juan and wanted to leave. I agreed. We walked back down the trail, the valley of Yécora spread out before us. It was twilight now, and the hills were shaded in purple and rose.

"Obviously when the humidity goes up, the hair curls, right?" George commented.

"Possibly. Who knows? At least that's what the Pimas believe."

"What happens to the food they leave?"

"That's a funny thing. It's always gone very soon after they leave it there. They think José Juan eats it. Do you want to go back and look?"

George got an odd look on his face. "No way. I don't like dead people, especially ones that have been dead for hundreds of years. That cave gives me the creeps. Let's go see if there's some supper ready."

He charged on ahead of me down the trail. I smiled and followed him. We had to leave in the morning, and I think all of us hated to go. This trip, like the others, had generated among us a closeness and comradeship that was hard to find in our day-to-day lives, where so many responsibilities tugged at us.

That night our songs were quiet ones, mainly the plaintive tunes of the *rancheros*. I was always sad to leave Yécora. I had become very close to Mac and appreciated his zest and enthusiasm for life. It seemed our visits were never long enough.

The next day we set out early for home and drove with relative ease over the narrow and dangerous road. The young men were asleep in the back, tired from our trip, or so I thought, when I heard a muffled sound behind me. I turned and saw that it was George.

Tears were streaming from his eyes, and his face was twisted with emotion. I knew his hard heart had cracked open, and the light I had hoped to find was shining out.

"Are you sorry to be leaving Yécora, George?" I asked softly.

He nodded. I reached a hand back and took his, gripping it firmly, hoping to communicate the love and understanding that filled my own heart. George closed his other hand around mine and held it tightly for a minute. Then he released it and turned his head to look out of the window for a last glimpse of the valley of Yécora.

My heart was full of gratitude, and tears stung my own eyes. As we came down out of the mountains, I knew that God's inner light had begun to shine.

Our trip out of Mexico was uneventful, except for our crossing of the border into the United States. Both the Mexican and American officials wanted to know what we had done with the rest of Ike's airplane, but finally we were across and on our way back to Tucson.

George's trip left us with a legacy. For as long as I visited the Sierra, I brought with me medical supplies for the Pima. George—a changed person—became a close friend and accompanied me on subsequent visits.

The story of the mummy of Yécora has a sequel. The next year when I returned to Yécora, Mac told me that an archaeologist from the University of Sonora had heard about their mummy.

"He came and took José Juan away! Do something about it, Pat. The Pimas don't know when to plant their crops." His face was lined with distress. "I've tried to tell them they don't really need José Juan, but they don't believe me. Will you help us?"

"I'll do what I can, Mac, but I'm not sure they'd listen to me either."

"It's one of the reasons I live away from cities. The people there are just plain mean!" Mac stomped off into the house.

On my way home, I visited the museum officials at the University of Sonora. I met with a small man in a suit and a tie, a very impertinent sort of fellow, who acted as if I had no appreciation for the importance of preserving relics such as José Juan.

"The mummy stays here. It's a treasure for everyone to enjoy."

"But he belongs to the Pima Indians. José Juan was a part of their rituals, and they sincerely believe that he told them when to plant their crops. If they plant too early, the squash seed will sprout. They need him, and they've taken care of him for at least a hundred years."

"The mummy belongs in the museum," he insisted.

"But don't you understand? He takes care of them."

His eyebrows rose. "Surely you don't believe those Indians?"

I could feel a hot flush creeping up my face. I was getting really angry. "What I believe isn't the point. The Pimas believe it, and they need José Juan to tell them when to plant."

"I'm sorry, but the mummy stays. Now I have important things to do. Good-bye."

I went back to my friends at the Casa de los Estudiantes, gloomy over the outcome of my visit.

"There must be something we can do," Jesús Lizárraga said to me.

"If there is, I don't know what it might be. The man says the mummy stays in the museum."

"At least we can protest!" Jesús said.

That night after the museum closed and the staff had gone home, a little band of us crept into the museum with the help of a sympathetic janitor. The next day when the first visitors

came in, they saw this placard in Spanish in front of the
mummy.

> My name is José Juan.
> You have been very wrong to take me from my cave.
> You shouldn't have taken me away.
> I tell the Pimas when to plant their crops.

Our protest was made, and I felt better about it, but José
Juan is still in the museum at the University of Sonora.

CHAPTER 14

The "I Don't Know" Indians

In the fall of 1958, I made another visit to Yécora in response to Mac's urgent request for some supplies. I had brought with me on this trip Gilberto Fierro, the talented young artist from the University of Sonora, Ivan Clark, the minister from Oklahoma, and José García, whom we picked up along the way. When the four of us arrived in Yécora, Mac looked sick and said he had been having some kidney trouble. As we relaxed and talked with Mac that night, he told us the legend of how the Pima Indians got their name.

◆ ◆

In the years just before 1600, a Spanish *conquistador* first rode through what is now the valley of Yécora. There he encountered a band of Pima Indians. They were awed by the sudden appearance of the bearded white man, and many of them fell to the ground. Others spread branches in his path, thinking he was a god.

In a haughty tone the *conquistador* asked, "Who are you?"

The Pimas did not understand Spanish and answered him in their own language. "*P'ema P'ishe e ma ah ah. P'ish e mah ah,*" they replied, which was their way of saying, "We don't understand you but we'd like to be friends. Please don't be so gruff with us."

The *conquistador* called to his scribe from the rear of the column. "The name of these people shall be recorded as the Pima Indians!" he commanded.

The scribe recorded on that day that the people of that region were the Pimas. The modern Pimas have carried this story forward from that time, and call themselves the "I don't know" tribe.

The Pimas' encounter with the Spaniards was to be nearly fatal for the Indians. The *conquistadores* rounded them up like cattle, put them in a pen, and then used them to replace the mules and horses that had died on the long trek north. Many Pimas died on their trip into what is now southern Arizona, and it was not long before the water almost ran out for the entire expedition. When the supply neared an end, the Pimas were the first to be denied the remaining water and began to die in great numbers.

Finally a group of them bolted and found water at the Gila River to the north. They followed its banks, which in those days were lined with bulrushes and cottonwoods, to the area of what is now Gila Bend. They eventually settled along the

Salt and Gila rivers, and today their descendants still live in this area of Arizona.

◆   ◆

Before going to sleep that night, Gilberto, Ivan, and I made plans to visit several Pima families, among them, the family of Luis Duarte, whom I had met on an earlier visit. In the morning, Mac gave us directions to the Duarte home.

Luis and his wife lived in a miserable little shack that was freezing cold in the winter. The walls and roofs of the Pima houses are inadequate against the harsh wind and rain. The Duarte house, like all Pima houses, was heated by an open fire on the dirt floor in its center.

I had taken Gilberto to meet the Duarte family because I wanted him to sketch a portrait of the Duarte's six-year-old son, Francisco, whom everyone called Pancho. When I had first met Pancho, he was unwashed, with a winsome face and an old, dirty flour sack for a shirt. He wore tiny jeans consisting of more patches than original cloth. Somehow his wistful eyes and enquiring expression seemed to speak to me, and I resolved to come back with Gilberto.

After greeting the family, I asked if Gilberto might sketch a picture of their son. This created great excitement on their part, and soon we were sitting around in front of their house on convenient hunks of wood or rocks, watching as Gilberto worked his magic with the charcoal pencil. Pancho was delighted and the portrait shows the wide grin that never left his face. His father, mother, older brother, all of the students who had come with me, and José García were watching. Young Pancho stood up well as the focus of all of this attention, and was not at all shy.

As we waited for Gilberto to finish his sketch, I studied the family's house and wondered why more effort wasn't taken to make it weatherproof. This particular one literally had been thrown together against the trunk of a pine tree, and significant holes were left unchinked against the winter winds, which were quite cold. Luis and his wife had produced nine children, yet only two were still living. This high mortality rate among the Pimas is typical. All the babies I saw had running noses or coughs. The few who survive beyond the age of three usually "make it."

When we returned to Mac's house that night, we talked more about the poverty and hardship among the Pima Indians. Mac told us about a sixteen-year-old young man who had epilepsy, a disease common among the Pimas. One day, while suffering an attack, the boy rolled into a fire and suffered terrible burns.

Mac also talked about the problem of alcoholism among the Indians. One man killed his child after drinking too much *mescal*, a potent liquor made by the Indians. One night the Pima man picked up his young son and threw him head first into a pine tree to stop him from crying. The child died from his injuries, one more fatality in the inexorable decline of this once-proud Indian nation. They probably numbered in the tens of thousands when Coronado came. Yet during my visits to their region, fewer than one thousand still lived. It was to these Indians that we were able to offer only a small amount of help.

CHAPTER 15

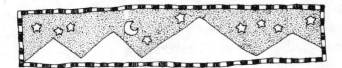

The Legend of the Pimas

The fire crackled in the hearth as we settled back against our bedrolls. Mac was in a story-telling mood that night, and Gilberto and Ivan were eager listeners. "How did the Pima Indians happen to settle in this area?" Ivan asked.

"The old men tell me that the Pima tribe came to Mexico, to the region of the Colorado delta, from a cold and snowy place far to the north. They settled in the place where the Colorado River runs into the sea and made their home there.

"When the Pimas arrived, other tribes had come before them—mostly farmers and hunters. They lived at peace with their brothers and considered each other to be descended from the same Totem or Great Spirit, personified by Laik, their supreme king."

Mac's voice took on a rolling, rhythmic tone as he continued. The log fell into the fire, sending a little shower of sparks into the room. I felt myself fall under the spell of his story.

"Laik was descended from Tashk, the sun god, who looked like a bearded white man and was their first deity and ruler. The Pima lived on fish from the river and the sea, and they raised corn, beans, and squash, which grew easily in the rich soil of the delta. They harvested vegetables, nuts, leaves, and fruits called *kikus*. They never suffered from famine or hunger. The delta was covered with forests, and they hunted animals and wild fowl. The Pimas were happy there, and their god stayed with them.

"The legend says they lived there for a long time, probably many centuries, until one day their god, Tashk, released Bainhamat Kgths, the god of darkness, who came upon them accompanied by hordes of evil spirits, producing storms that were frightful in their intensity. Then came earthquakes, tremendous shakings of the earth, making their houses fall down.

"As a testimony of this, the elders of the tribe point to the cataclysm of the rise of the Pinacate volcano with its huge lava flow, as well as the sinking of their great valley and the formation of the Gulf of California. These disasters caused many deaths and losses and made life impossible in the delta area. The people knew they had to migrate, to leave their homes and find another home."

Mac rose from his chair and stirred the fire, his eyes sparkling in the firelight.

"Many tribes left the delta. The Yaqui and the Mayo tribes went south, toward the eastern deserts and the Mexican coast. The Tarahumaras climbed the Sierra Madre and spread out into the high mountain valleys, where they farmed, hunted, and mined for gold and silver."

"Gold? Silver? I didn't know they were miners," Gilberto said. All the young people were interested in this. The lure of lost gold mines had an appeal that transcended age and nationality, or so I had noticed every time the subject came up.

Mac smiled, pleased at having the keen interest of his audience, and went on. "When the Spanish explorers arrived on the scene in the sixteenth century, they found the headquarters of the Pima tribes approximately thirty miles northeast of the present-day town of Nuri, Sonora. It was located at a place the tribe called Ostimuri, near the Río Chico—not far from the Yaqui River. The ruins of this first capital are still there, or so the Pimas say. I've not seen them myself. Ostimuri was famous for its gold-smelting and silver-plating arts. The metal workers of the Pimas made beautiful jewelry and gold ornaments for their own use."

"Was that the only city?" Ivan asked.

"No, there were many old villages. Ostimuri, Ures, and Vaviape; Tepache, Maicova, Tezopaco, and Santa Rosa; Nuri, Arivechi, and Sahuaripa; Nacori Grande, Suaquí, San Rafael, and San José de Pimas. They also founded Bana-miche, Baviácora, and Cucurpe. They once inhabited half of Sonora and founded many of the towns of the state."

"Tell me more about the gold," Gilberto said, leaning forward.

"Let me tell you more about the tribe," Mac said gently. "Then I'll tell you about the gold."

"All right," Gilberto said and settled back again.

"The people lived in clusters of a few families each and made themselves homes, farmed, and hunted. Each group had its own subchief, or Tahwaeak, who was a deputy for the

Lord Chief Laik, who lived in Ostimuri. Laik, who represented Tashk in human form, held absolute and indisputable authority, which he received through inheritance. The subchiefs were named directly by Laik and reigned from four to ten years, according to their effectiveness."

"How did the subchief keep control of the people?" I asked.

"By means of salt. Only the subchief had the tribe's salt, which he gathered once a year from salt beds near the seacoast. At the time of each full moon, the families would gather for their distribution of salt, and by means of this, the government was maintained."

"Did they have crime?" Ivan asked.

"Yes. In case of crime, the severity of the punishment varied according to the seriousness of the offense. If the crime was robbery, the penalty was to repay double the amount of the theft. For murder, the criminal was executed in the same manner as his victim. For a light offense, hard labor in the salt beds was the sentence. A woman suspected of adultery was taken to the mountains and left absolutely alone for six moons. If she could prove her innocence after that time, she would be welcomed back. Otherwise she would be ravished and expelled from the tribe, after the authorities had placed on her scalp a chemical that would prevent her hair from growing. Even members of other tribes looked upon such unfortunates with scorn."

"What about tribal wars? Was there fighting among the tribes?" Ivan asked.

"Sometimes. In the case of war, all males from age sixteen to fifty were obliged to go. Because there was no regular band of warriors, all the men stayed in training and were skillful and obedient when the call came."

"We keep hearing about the Pima festivals. Tell us about those," Gilberto requested.

"The legend says their gods are Tashk, the sun god of strong men and good harvests, and Masht, the moon goddess, who is worshiped by the women every twenty-eight days in a ceremony to which no men are invited. Unfortunately the Pimas had witch doctors, and one of these, along with the chief, was in charge of the sacrificing of three-year-old children. These children were always the offspring of a high government official, and their tears after a prolonged death by hunger, thirst, and grief were said to represent rain that their rain god Chorsam would then send to the people."

The room was silent for a long time, as we digested this story.

"What happened to their gold? The people around here don't seem to have any," Gilberto said.

"The mines are still all around in the hills. Of course the Spaniards took them all as soon as they were found. It's a hard life now for most of the Pimas. I suppose if there had been any substantial amount of gold in the form of ornaments, it went on mules back to the king."

"So that's the legend of the Pimas," Gilberto said, his face thoughtful.

"That's the legend as it was told to me. Now I think I need some sleep." Mac heaved himself to his feet. "I'm an old man now. Good night to you all. Have a pleasant sleep."

CHAPTER 16

Sowing White Roses in the Heart

It was a crisp afternoon in the fall of 1959. I was sitting in my garden in Tucson, watching the flashing feathers of a cardinal in the palo verde tree when Julia brought me a letter. It was postmarked Yécora, and it was addressed in a handwriting I didn't recognize. A shiver of fear passed through me. Mac was the only person who had ever written me from Yécora, and he hadn't been well the last time I had seen him.

I had gone to Yécora at Easter and had recently written Mac to tell him I would be spending the Thanksgiving holiday at home this year, but I would plan a trip to see him between Christmas and New Year's.

In his last letter he had told me that he was recovering

slowly from some surgery he had had in Obregón. He had been forced to stay for a time in a home in Tezopaco so that he could be nearer to medical attention. Mac hated to be sick. I had been concerned, but I wasn't terribly worried about it.

I turned over the envelope and slit open the flap.

Dear *Señor* Jenks,

Your dear friend Gordon McMurray has died in his sleep. He had not been feeling well for a long time and came home to be near the people he loved. I am writing you this on behalf of all of us who cared about him, because we know that you loved him too and would want to know that he has gone. We've buried him on the hill where the pine trees start and have put some big rocks on the grave, so you can find it when you come. We miss him very much.

The people here have asked me to tell you that we have been grateful for the help you have given to all of us. Our life is much better than it was when you started to come down here. *Usted está sembrando rosas blancas en el corazón de los Mexicanos* [You are sowing white roses in the hearts of the Mexican people]. We thank you for this and pray that you and your family are well.

The letter was signed by one of the people who lived near Mac. I felt tears sting my eyes and let them flow. My voice shook as I turned to Julia. "Mac's gone. He's died at home in Yécora." I felt that emptiness that seems to come to me when I've suffered a loss, and I knew from experience it would be with me for a while.

Julia came to where I was sitting and put her arms around me. "I'm so sorry, Pat. I know he was a dear friend."

Winter came, and the Christmas season passed without my making a visit to Yécora. In the spring, when I might have

been making plans for the trip, one of the children had some medical problems, and I postponed the trip again. It took me over a year to realize that I couldn't bear the idea of driving up that dusty road to Mac's house and find him gone. In my mind, he lives there still. I see him filling the doorway with his square form, a big smile on his grizzled face, and an arm in the air, waving a welcome to me as I leap from the jeep to greet him.

REFLECTIONS

The young people of today are the leaders of tomorrow. Lead them in the right direction—always to Christ, our Lord and Savior. This has been and *is* my maxim and my aim.

Life is truly wonderful when we can just throw away our worries and cares and march happily along from day to day, seeking to do a little good here and there, and then being able to rejoice quietly over the help we have been to someone, especially to a young person. Such joy God gives as his reward for our happy efforts in his direction, and it grows in intensity and frequency as it is multiplied.

One day last spring my soul was caught on a golden beam that took it to the other end of a rainbow nearby. There in a secluded canyon niche among towering peaks above, a crystal brook ran tinkling over moss-covered cliffs. Here were rubies, diamonds, emeralds—all the colors of the rainbow—caught in one scintillating creature, hovering, emanating the flow of all colors of the spectrum at the fabled pot of gold: a hummingbird drinking nectar from the golden tube, the handiwork of God.

A still, small voice said to me: "Here is your treasure, found. You no longer need to search. Your restless, mundane climb to wealth is all of no avail. I give your soul this heavenly glimpse to show you that more awaits you at the end of your life's toilsome trail. The rapture of the mountain mists with sunbeams streaming through; the ecstasy of this bright spot brings the peace of God to you."

Oh! But if we could impart to others this bright treasure trove—God's nature as is fashioned here, interpreted in love.

You cannot serve both God and wealth, dividing body, self, and creed. In such a life we find destruction, riot, chaos, war, and greed.

> *Redeem us, Savior.*
> *Thou art divine.*
>
> *In thy paths, Christians find*
> *True love, holiness, and power,*
> *Each and every day and hour.*
>
> *Lord, defender of our souls,*
> *Keep us straight and true.*
> *In the paths of righteousness,*
> *Help us follow through.*

Desert Quest was set in Goudy Old Style, a typeface
designed by Frederic W. Goudy in 1915 for ATF. The
type was set by the Composition Department of
Zondervan Publishing House, Sue Koppenol, compositor.
The interior design and chapter decorations are the work
of Ann Cherryman. The photo sections and the maps
were designed by Florence Chambers. The scratch-board
illustrations are by Mark Herron of the Aslan Group,
Ltd. The cover was designed by the Aslan Group, Ltd.
The book was printed by Arcata Graphics of
Martinsburg, West Virginia.